the writings

NEW INTERNATIONAL READER'S VERSION

THE BOOKS OF THE BIBLE

for kids

ZONDER**kidz**

NIrV, The Books of the Bible for Kids: The Writings
Copyright © 2017 by Biblica
Illustrations © 2017 by Zondervan

The Holy Bible, *New International Reader's Version*®
Copyright © 1995, 1996, 1998, 2014 by Biblica, Inc.®
All rights reserved

Published by Zonderkidz
3900 Sparks Dr. SE, Grand Rapids, Michigan 49546, U.S.A.

www.zonderkidz.com

Library of Congress Catalog Card Number 2017941836

Printed in the United States of America   NIrV 2014

17 18 19 20 21 22 23 24 25 /DCI/ 20 19 18 17 16 15 14 13 12 11 10 9 8 7 6 5 4 3 2

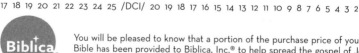

You will be pleased to know that a portion of the purchase price of your new NIrV Bible has been provided to Biblica, Inc.® to help spread the gospel of Jesus Christ around the world!

Contents

Introduction to The Writings 5

DAY 1: Psalms, part 1 7
DAY 2: Psalms, part 2 14
DAY 3: Psalms, part 3 22
DAY 4: Psalms, part 4 29
DAY 5: Psalms, part 5 36
DAY 6: Psalms, part 6 44
DAY 7: Psalms, part 7 51
DAY 8: Psalms, part 8 59
DAY 9: Psalms, part 9 66
DAY 10: Psalms, part 10 73
DAY 11: Psalms, part 11 80
DAY 12: Psalms, part 12 87
DAY 13: Psalms, part 13 94
DAY 14: Lamentations 102
DAY 15: Song of Songs 112
DAY 16: Proverbs, part 1 118
DAY 17: Proverbs, part 2 125
DAY 18: Proverbs, part 3 133
DAY 19: Proverbs, part 4 140
DAY 20: Ecclesiastes 148
DAY 21: Job, part 1 157
DAY 22: Job, part 2 165
DAY 23: Job, part 3 173
DAY 24: Job, part 4 181
DAY 25: Job, part 5 189
DAY 26: Chronicles, part 1 196
DAY 27: Chronicles, part 2 204
DAY 28: Chronicles, part 3 210
DAY 29: Chronicles, part 4 217
DAY 30: Chronicles, part 5 224
DAY 31: Chronicles, part 6 231

DAY 32: Chronicles, part 7 238

DAY 33: Chronicles, part 8 245

DAY 34: Chronicles, part 9 252

DAY 35: Ezra, part 2; Nehemiah, part 1 260

DAY 36: Nehemiah, part 2 267

DAY 37: Esther, part 1 274

DAY 38: Esther, part 2 280

DAY 39: Daniel, part 1 286

DAY 40: Daniel, part 2 295

A Word About the NIrV 303

introduction to The Writings

The Writings is a collection of books written many years ago. The Writings is part of a much bigger collection known as "the Bible."

Long ago, God created the world. Everything he made was good. But creation turned its back on God. Suddenly, the whole world was caught up in sin and death.

So God set out to rescue his good creation—to save us from sin and death. He promised a man named Abraham that his family would bring blessing to all nations and make things right.

Years later, God made a covenant, a very serious agreement, with Abraham's grandchildren's grandchildren. This agreement made these people a "kingdom of priests" and a "holy nation" for God. It taught them how to live well. They would help the world know and obey God. The covenant had promises called blessings for the nation if they obeyed God. It also promised curses if they disobeyed.

Sadly, the nation of Israel seemed to always live like the rest of the world, caught up in sin and death. Because one king disobeyed so badly, Israel split into two nations, Israel and Judah.

The Writings is full of different kinds of writing. It begins with poetry. These are often the words of songs. Sometimes the people sang to God because he was powerful and saved them. Other times they sang because they were sad and scared. It seems like they had a song for every situation in life. We can make these songs our own to give us words for our deep feelings.

Another kind of writing is wisdom. These are wise sayings and comments about life that are true most of the time. They describe how life seems to work, not that something will always be true.

Then there is history in the Writings. Chronicles–Ezra–Nehemiah tell the story of Israel from the beginning of time until the city of Jerusalem is rebuilt after the people returned from Babylon. It tells the same story as Genesis to Samuel–Kings, but in a different way.

The books of Esther and Daniel finish the Writings, and you will read more about them later.

PSALMS, PART 1

introduction to Psalms, parts 1-13

The book of Psalms is 150 songs. The writers and singers sang for different reasons. Sometimes they simply wanted to praise God because he is good and powerful and the true King of creation. Other times they wanted to thank God for giving them things and protecting them. Sometimes they needed something, so they sang their prayer to ask God to protect them or provide for them.

These three main types of psalms also had different purposes. A praise psalm might celebrate God's justice, his loving kindness, his care for creation, or his rule over creation. A prayer psalm might ask for forgiveness or healing. It might ask God to deliver the people from their enemies or to destroy their enemies. Israel even had psalms for special times. They sang at weddings or when they put the crown on a new king for the first time. They sang to commit themselves to God's laws again. They also sang as they climbed the steep hills into Jerusalem to worship God at the temple.

See if you can figure out what kind of psalm each one is as you read it.

Psalm 1

Blessed is the person who obeys the law of the Lord.
   They don't follow the advice of evil people.
They don't make a habit of doing what sinners do.
   They don't join those who make fun of the Lord and
      his law.

Instead, the law of the LORD gives them joy.
They think about his law day and night.
That kind of person is like a tree that is planted near a stream
of water.
It always bears its fruit at the right time.
Its leaves don't dry up.
Everything godly people do turns out well.

Sinful people are not like that at all.
They are like straw
that the wind blows away.
When the LORD judges them, their life will come to an end.
Sinners won't have any place among those who are godly.

The LORD watches over the lives of godly people.
But the lives of sinful people will lead to their death.

Psalm 2

Why do the nations plan evil together?
Why do they make useless plans?
The kings of the earth rise up against the LORD.
The rulers of the earth join together against his anointed
king.
"Let us break free from their chains," they say.
"Let us throw off their ropes."

The God who sits on his throne in heaven laughs.
The Lord makes fun of those rulers and their plans.
When he is angry, he warns them.
When his anger blazes out, he terrifies them.
He says to them,
"I have placed my king on my holy mountain of Zion."

I will announce what the LORD has promised.

He said to me, "You are my son.
Today I have become your father.
Ask me, and I will give the nations to you.
All nations on earth will belong to you.

You will break them with an iron scepter.
  You will smash them to pieces like clay pots."

Kings, be wise!
  Rulers of the earth, be warned!
  Serve the LORD and have respect for him.
    Celebrate his rule with trembling.
Obey the son completely, or he will be angry.
  Your way of life will lead to your death.
His anger can blaze out at any moment.
  Blessed are all those who go to him for safety.

Psalm 4

For the director of music. A psalm of David to
be played on stringed instruments.

My faithful God,
  answer me when I call out to you.
Give me rest from my trouble.
  Have mercy on me. Hear my prayer.

How long will you people turn my glory into shame?
  How long will you love what will certainly fail you?
  How long will you pray to statues of gods?
Remember that the LORD has set apart his faithful servant for
    himself.
  The LORD hears me when I call out to him.

Tremble and do not sin.
  When you are in bed,
  look deep down inside yourself and be silent.
Offer to the LORD the sacrifices that godly people offer.
  Trust in him.

LORD, many are asking, "Who will make us successful?"
  LORD, may you do good things for us.
Fill my heart with joy
  when the people have lots of grain and fresh wine.
In peace I will lie down and sleep.
  LORD, you alone keep me safe.

Psalm 8

For the director of music. According to gittith. *A psalm of David.*

LORD, our Lord,
  how majestic is your name in the whole earth!
You have set your glory
  in the heavens.
You have made sure that children
  and infants praise you.
Their praise is a wall
  that stops the talk of your enemies.

I think about the heavens.
  I think about what your fingers have created.
I think about the moon and stars
  that you have set in place.
What are human beings that you think about them?
  What is a son of man that you take care of him?
You have made them a little lower than the angels.
  You placed on them a crown of glory and honor.

You made human beings rule over everything your hands
    created.
  You put everything under their control.
They rule over all flocks and herds
  and over the wild animals.
They rule over the birds in the sky
  and over the fish in the ocean.
  They rule over everything that swims in the oceans.

LORD, our Lord,
  how majestic is your name in the whole earth!

Psalm 11

For the director of music. A psalm of David.

I run to the LORD for safety.
  So how can you say to me,
  "Fly away like a bird to your mountain.

Look! Evil people are bending their bows.
　　They are placing their arrows against the strings.
　　They are planning to shoot from the shadows
　　　　at those who have honest hearts.
　　When law and order are being destroyed,
　　　　what can godly people do?"

The Lord is in his holy temple.
　　The Lord is on his throne in heaven.
　　He watches everyone on earth.
　　　　His eyes study them.
The Lord watches over those who do what is right.
　　But he really hates sinful people and those who love to hurt
　　　　others.
He will pour out flaming coals and burning sulfur
　　on those who do what is wrong.
　　A hot and dry wind will destroy them.

The Lord always does what is right.
　　So he loves it when people do what is fair.
　　Those who are honest will enjoy his blessing.

Psalm 17

A prayer of David.

Lord, hear me, because I ask for what is right.
　　Listen to my cry for help.
Hear my prayer.
　　It doesn't come from lips that tell lies.
When you hand down your sentence, may it be in my favor.
　　May your eyes see what is right.

Look deep down into my heart.
　　Study me carefully at night and test me.
　　You won't find anything wrong.
I have planned nothing evil.
　　My mouth has not said sinful things.
Though evil people tried to pay me to do wrong,
　　I have not done what they wanted.

Instead I have done what you commanded.
My steps have stayed on your paths.
My feet have not slipped.

My God, I call out to you because you will answer me.
Listen to me. Hear my prayer.
Show me the wonders of your great love.
By using your great power,
you save those who go to you for safety from their enemies.
Take good care of me, just as you would take care of your
own eyes.
Hide me in the shadow of your wings.
Save me from the sinful people who want to destroy me.
Save me from my deadly enemies who are all around me.

They make their hearts hard and stubborn.
Their mouths speak with pride.
They have tracked me down. They are all around me.
Their eyes watch for a chance to throw me to the ground.
They are like a hungry lion, waiting to attack.
They are like a powerful lion, hiding in the bushes.

LORD, rise up. Oppose them and bring them down.
With your sword, save me from those evil people.
LORD, by your power save me from people like that.
They belong to this world. They get their reward in this life.

May what you have stored up for evil people fill their bellies.
May their children's stomachs be filled with it.
And may there even be leftovers for their little ones.
You will show that I am right; I will enjoy your blessing.
When I wake up, I will be satisfied because I will see you.

remember what you read

1. What is something you noticed for the first time?

That we can use some of the Psalms in our prayers

2. What questions did you have?

None

3. Was there anything that bothered you?

No

4. What did you learn about loving God?

That God loves us & the people who obey his law.

5. What did you learn about loving others?

That we could use Psalms 17 to encourage others that God will protect them in their hard times

PSALMS, PART 2

Psalm 19

For the director of music. A psalm of David.

The heavens tell about the glory of God.
   The skies show that his hands created them.
Day after day they speak about it.
   Night after night they make it known.
But they don't speak or use words.
   No sound is heard from them.
Yet their voice goes out into the whole earth.
   Their words go out from one end of the world to the other.

God has set up a tent in the heavens for the sun.
   The sun is like a groom leaving the room of his wedding
      night.
   The sun is like a great runner who takes delight in running
      a race.
It rises at one end of the heavens.
   Then it moves across to the other end.
   Everything enjoys its warmth.

The law of the Lord is perfect.
   It gives us new strength.
The laws of the Lord can be trusted.
   They make childish people wise.
The rules of the Lord are right.
   They give joy to our hearts.
The commands of the Lord shine brightly.
   They give light to our minds.

The law that brings respect for the LORD is pure.
It lasts forever.
The commands the LORD gives are true.
All of them are completely right.
They are more priceless than gold.
They have greater value than huge amounts of pure
gold.
They are sweeter than honey
that is taken from the honeycomb.
Your servant is warned by them.
When people obey them, they are greatly rewarded.

But who can know their own mistakes?
Forgive my hidden faults.
Also keep me from the sins I want to commit.
May they not be my master.
Then I will be without blame.
I will not be guilty of any great sin against your
law.

LORD, may these words of my mouth please you.
And may these thoughts of my heart please you also.
You are my Rock and my Redeemer.

Psalm 20

For the director of music. A psalm of David.

May the LORD answer you when you are in trouble.
May the God of Jacob keep you safe.
May he send you help from the sacred tent.
May he give you aid from Zion.
May he remember all your sacrifices.
May he accept your burnt offerings.
May he give you what your heart wishes for.
May he make all your plans succeed.
May we shout for joy over your victory.
May we lift up our flags in the name of our God.
May the LORD give you everything you ask for.

Now I know that the LORD gives victory to his anointed
 king.
He answers him from his sacred home in heaven.
The power of God's right hand gives victory to the
 king.
Some trust in chariots. Some trust in horses.
 But we trust in the LORD our God.
They are brought to their knees and fall down.
 But we get up and stand firm.

LORD, give victory to the king!
 Answer us when we call out to you!

Psalm 23

A psalm of David.

The LORD is my shepherd. He gives me everything
 I need.
He lets me lie down in fields of green grass.
He leads me beside quiet waters.
 He gives me new strength.
He guides me in the right paths
 for the honor of his name.
Even though I walk
 through the darkest valley,
I will not be afraid.
 You are with me.
Your shepherd's rod and staff
 comfort me.

You prepare a feast for me
 right in front of my enemies.
You pour oil on my head.
 My cup runs over.
I am sure that your goodness and love will follow me
 all the days of my life.
And I will live in the house of the LORD
 forever.

Psalm 24

A psalm of David.

The earth belongs to the LORD. And so does everything in it.
The world belongs to him. And so do all those who live in it.
He set it firmly on the oceans.
He made it secure on the waters.

Who can go up to the temple on the mountain of the
    LORD?
Who can stand in his holy place?
Anyone who has clean hands and a pure heart.
    Anyone who does not trust in the statue of a god.
    Anyone who doesn't use the name of that god when he
        makes a promise.
People like that will receive the LORD's blessing.
    When God their Savior hands down his sentence, it will
        be in their favor.
The people who look to God are like that.
    God of Jacob, they look to you.

Open wide, you gates.
    Open up, you ancient doors.
    Then the King of glory will come in.
Who is the King of glory?
    The LORD, who is strong and mighty.
    The LORD, who is mighty in battle.
Open wide, you gates.
    Open wide, you ancient doors.
    Then the King of glory will come in.
Who is he, this King of glory?
    The LORD who rules over all.
    He is the King of glory.

Psalm 27

A psalm of David.

The LORD is my light, and he saves me.
    Why should I fear anyone?

The LORD is my place of safety.
    Why should I be afraid?
My enemies are evil.
    They will trip and fall
when they attack me
    and try to swallow me up.
Even if an army attacks me,
    my heart will not be afraid.
Even if war breaks out against me,
    I will still trust in God.

I'm asking the LORD for only one thing.
    Here is what I want.
I want to live in the house of the LORD
    all the days of my life.
I want to look at the beauty of the LORD.
    I want to worship him in his temple.
When I'm in trouble,
    he will keep me safe in his house.
He will hide me in the safety of his holy tent.
    He will put me on a rock that is very high.
Then I will win the battle
    over my enemies who are all around me.
At his holy tent I will offer my sacrifice with shouts
        of joy.
    I will sing and make music to the LORD.

LORD, hear my voice when I call out to you.
    Treat me with kindness and answer me.
My heart says, "Seek him!"
    LORD, I will seek you.
Don't turn your face away from me.
    Don't turn me away because you are angry.
    You have helped me.
God my Savior, don't say no to me.
    Don't desert me.
My father and mother may desert me,
    but the LORD will accept me.

Lord, teach me your ways.
  Lead me along a straight path.
  There are many people who treat me badly.
My enemies want to harm me. So don't turn me over to them.
  Witnesses who tell lies are rising up against me.
  They say all sorts of evil things about me.

Here is something I am still sure of.
  I will see the Lord's goodness
  while I'm still alive.
Wait for the Lord.
  Be strong and don't lose hope.
Wait for the Lord.

Psalm 29

A psalm of David.

Praise the Lord, you angels in heaven.
  Praise the Lord for his glory and strength.
Praise the Lord for the glory that belongs to him.
  Worship the Lord because of his beauty and holiness.

The voice of the Lord is heard over the waters.
  The God of glory thunders.
  The Lord thunders over the mighty waters.
The voice of the Lord is powerful.
  The voice of the Lord is majestic.
The voice of the Lord breaks the cedar trees.
  The Lord breaks the cedars of Lebanon into pieces.
He makes the mountains of Lebanon leap like a calf.
  He makes Mount Hermon jump like a young wild ox.
The voice of the Lord strikes
  with flashes of lightning.
The voice of the Lord shakes the desert.
  The Lord shakes the Desert of Kadesh.
The voice of the Lord twists the oak trees.
  It strips the forests bare.
  And in his temple everyone cries out, "Glory!"

The LORD on his throne rules over the flood.
The LORD rules from his throne as King forever.
The LORD gives strength to his people.
The LORD blesses his people with peace.

remember what you read

1. What is something you noticed for the first time?

That instead of think thunderstorms are scary I now see them as God's glory.

2. What questions did you have?

None.

3. Was there anything that bothered you?

No.

4. What did you learn about loving God?

That God is an amazing God. He rules over everything including us. So because He is our Creator all of our Glory should go to him.

5. What did you learn about loving others?

That we could use Psalm 23 to encourage others in they are going through a hard time.

Psalm 30

*A psalm of David. A song for setting apart
the completed temple to God.*

LORD, I will give you honor.
 You brought me out of deep trouble.
 You didn't give my enemies the joy of seeing me die.
LORD my God, I called out to you for help.
 And you healed me.
LORD, you brought me up from the place of the dead.
 You kept me from going down into the pit.

Sing the praises of the LORD, you who are faithful to him.
 Praise him, because his name is holy.
His anger lasts for only a moment.
 But his favor lasts for a person's whole life.
Weeping can stay for the night.
 But joy comes in the morning.

When I felt safe, I said,
 "I will always be secure."
LORD, when you gave me your help,
 you made Mount Zion stand firm.
But when you took away your help,
 I was terrified.

LORD, I called out to you.
 I cried to you for mercy.
I said, "What good will come if I become silent in death?
 What good will come if I go down into the grave?

Can the dust of my dead body praise you?
  Can it tell how faithful you are?
LORD, hear me. Have mercy on me.
  LORD, help me."

You turned my loud crying into dancing.
  You removed my clothes of sadness and dressed me
    with joy.
So my heart will sing your praises. I can't keep silent.
  LORD, my God, I will praise you forever.

Psalm 31

For the director of music. A psalm of David.

LORD, I have come to you for safety.
  Don't let me ever be put to shame.
  Save me, because you do what is right.
Pay attention to me.
  Come quickly to help me.
Be the rock I go to for safety.
  Be the strong fort that saves me.
You are my rock and my fort.
  Lead me and guide me for the honor of your name.
Keep me free from the trap that is set for me.
  You are my place of safety.
Into your hands I commit my very life.
  LORD, set me free. You are my faithful God.

I hate those who worship worthless statues of gods.
  But I trust in the LORD.
I will be glad and full of joy because you love me.
  You saw that I was hurting.
  You took note of my great pain.
You have not handed me over to the enemy.
  You have put me in a wide and safe place.

LORD, have mercy on me. I'm in deep trouble.
  I'm so sad I can hardly see.
  My whole body grows weak with sadness.

Pain has taken over my life.
  My years are spent in groaning.
I have no strength because I'm hurting so much.
  My body is getting weaker and weaker.
My neighbors make fun of me
  because I have so many enemies.
My closest friends are afraid of me.
  People who see me on the street run away
      from me.
No one remembers me. I might as well be dead.
  I have become like broken pottery.
I hear many people whispering,
  "There is terror all around him!"
Many have joined together against me.
  They plan to kill me.

But I trust in you, LORD.
  I say, "You are my God."
My whole life is in your hands.
  Save me from the hands of my enemies.
  Save me from those who are chasing me.
May you look on me with favor.
  Save me because your love is faithful.
LORD, I have cried out to you.
  Don't let me be put to shame.
But let sinners be put to shame.
  Let them lie silent in the place of the dead.
Their lips tell lies. Let them be silenced.
  They speak with pride against those who do right.
  They make fun of them.

You have stored up so many good things.
  You have stored them up for those who have respect
      for you.
You give those things while everyone watches.
  You give them to people who run to you for safety.
They are safe because you are with them.
  You hide them from the evil plans of their enemies.

In your house you keep them safe
 from those who bring charges against them.

Give praise to the Lord.
 He showed me his wonderful love
 when my enemies attacked the city I was in.
I was afraid and said,
 "I've been cut off from you!"
But you heard my cry for your favor.
 You heard me when I called out to you for help.

Love the Lord, all you who are faithful to him!
 The Lord keeps safe those who are faithful to him.
 But he completely pays back those who are proud.
Be strong, all you who put your hope in the Lord.
 Never give up.

Psalm 32

A maskil of David.

Blessed is the person whose lawless acts are forgiven.
 Their sins have been taken away.
Blessed is the person whose sin the Lord never counts
  against them.
 That person doesn't want to cheat anyone.

When I kept silent about my sin,
 my body became weak
 because I groaned all day long.
Day and night
 you punished me.
I became weaker and weaker
 as I do in the heat of summer.
Then I admitted my sin to you.
 I didn't cover up the wrong I had done.
I said, "I will admit my lawless acts to the Lord."
 And you forgave the guilt of my sin.

Let everyone who is faithful pray to you
 while they can still look to you.

When troubles come like a flood,
   they certainly won't reach those who are faithful.
You are my hiding place.
   You will keep me safe from trouble.
You will surround me with songs sung by those who
      praise you
   because you save your people.

I will guide you and teach you the way you should go.
   I will give you good advice and watch over you with love.
Don't be like a horse or a mule.
   They can't understand anything.
They have to be controlled by bits and bridles.
   If they aren't, they won't come to you.
Sinful people have all kinds of trouble.
   But the LORD's faithful love
   is all around those who trust in him.

Be glad because of what the LORD has done for you.
   Be joyful, you who do what is right!
   Sing, all you whose hearts are honest!

Psalm 34

A psalm of David when he was with Abimelek and pretended to be
out of his mind. Abimelek drove him away, and David left.

I will thank the LORD at all times.
   My lips will always praise him.
I will find my glory in knowing the LORD.
   Let those who are hurting hear me and be joyful.
Join me in giving glory to the LORD.
   Let us honor him together.

I looked to the LORD, and he answered me.
   He saved me from everything I was afraid of.
Those who look to him have joyful faces.
   They are never covered with shame.
This poor man called out, and the LORD heard him.
   He saved him out of all his troubles.

The angel of the LORD stands guard
  around those who have respect for him.
  And he saves them.

Taste and see that the LORD is good.
  Blessed is the person who goes to him for safety.
You holy people of God, have respect for the LORD.
  Those who respect him have everything they need.
The lions may grow weak and hungry.
  But those who look to the LORD have every good thing they
    need.

My children, come. Listen to me.
  I will teach you to have respect for the LORD.
Do you love life
  and want to see many good days?
Then keep your tongues from speaking evil.
  Keep your lips from telling lies.
Turn away from evil, and do good.
  Look for peace, and go after it.

The LORD looks with favor on those who are godly.
  His ears are open to their cry.
But the LORD doesn't look with favor on those who do evil.
  He removes all memory of them from the earth.

Godly people cry out, and the LORD hears them.
  He saves them from all their troubles.
The LORD is close to those whose hearts have been broken.
  He saves those whose spirits have been crushed.

The person who does what is right may have many troubles.
  But the LORD saves him from all of them.
The LORD watches over all his bones.
  Not one of them will be broken.

Sinners will be killed by their own evil.
  The enemies of godly people will be judged.
The LORD will save those who serve him.
  No one who goes to him for safety will be found guilty.

remember what you read

1. What is something you noticed for the first time?

That God will save those who come to him for safty in time of war.

2. What questions did you have?

None.

3. Was there anything that bothered you?

No.

4. What did you learn about loving God?

That if you addmit your sins to God he will forgive you.

5. What did you learn about loving others?

That we can use Psalm 30 to comfort people if they feel like they won't make it through their troubles.

Psalm 42–43

For the director of music. A maskil *of the Sons of Korah.*

A deer longs for streams of water.
  God, I long for you in the same way.
I am thirsty for God. I am thirsty for the living God.
  When can I go and meet with him?
My tears have been my food
  day and night.
All day long people say to me,
  "Where is your God?"
When I remember what has happened,
  I tell God all my troubles.
I remember how I used to walk to the house of God.
  The Mighty One guarded my steps.
We shouted with joy and praised God
  as we went along with the joyful crowd.

My spirit, why are you so sad?
  Why are you so upset deep down inside me?
Put your hope in God.
  Once again I will have reason to praise him.
  He is my Savior and my God.

My spirit is very sad deep down inside me.
  So I will remember you here where the Jordan River
    begins.
I will remember you here on the Hermon mountains
  and on Mount Mizar.

You have sent wave upon wave of trouble over me.
    It roars down on me like a waterfall.
All your waves and breakers have rolled over me.

During the day the LORD sends his love to me.
    During the night I sing about him.
    I say a prayer to the God who gives me life.

I say to God my Rock,
    "Why have you forgotten me?
Why must I go around in sorrow?
    Why am I treated so badly by my enemies?"
My body suffers deadly pain
    as my enemies make fun of me.
All day long they say to me,
    "Where is your God?"

My spirit, why are you so sad?
    Why are you so upset deep down inside me?
Put your hope in God.
    Once again I will have reason to praise him.
    He is my Savior and my God.

My God, when you hand down your decision, let it be in my
        favor.
    Stand up for me against an unfaithful nation.
    Save me from those lying and sinful people.
You are God, my place of safety.
    Why have you turned your back on me?
Why must I go around in sorrow?
    Why am I beaten down by my enemies?
Send me your light and your faithful care.
    Let them lead me.
Let them bring me back to your holy mountain,
    to the place where you live.
Then I will go to the altar of God.
    I will go to God. He is my joy and my delight.
God, you are my God.
    I will praise you by playing the lyre.

My spirit, why are you so sad?
    Why are you so upset deep down inside me?
Put your hope in God.
    Once again I will have reason to praise him.
    He is my Savior and my God.

Psalm 45

*For the director of music. A maskil of the Sons of
Korah. A wedding song to the tune of "Lilies."*

My heart is full of beautiful words
    as I say my poem for the king.
    My tongue is like the pen of a skillful writer.

You are the most excellent of men.
    Your lips have been given the ability to speak gracious
        words.
    God has blessed you forever.
Mighty one, put your sword at your side.
    Put on glory and majesty as if they were your clothes.
In your majesty ride out with power
    to fight for what is true, humble and fair.
    Let your right hand do wonderful things.
Shoot your sharp arrows into the hearts of your enemies.
    Let the nations come under your control.
Your throne is the very throne of God.
    Your kingdom will last for ever and ever.
    You will rule by treating everyone fairly.
You love what is right and hate what is evil.
    So your God has placed you above your companions.
    He has filled you with joy by pouring the sacred oil on your
        head.
Myrrh and aloes and cassia make all your robes smell good.
    In palaces decorated with ivory
    the music played on stringed instruments makes you glad.
Daughters of kings are among the women you honor.
    At your right hand is the royal bride dressed in gold from
        Ophir.

Royal bride, listen and pay careful attention.
  Forget about your people and the home you came from.
Let the king be charmed by your beauty.
  Honor him. He is now your master.
The people of Tyre will come with gifts.
  Wealthy people will try to gain your favor.

In her room, the princess looks glorious.
  Her gown has gold threads running through it.
Dressed in beautiful clothes, she is led to the king.
  Her virgin companions follow her.
  They have been brought to be with her.
They are led in with joy and gladness.
  They enter the palace of the king.

Your sons will rule just as your father and grandfather did.
  You will make them princes through the whole land.
I will make sure that people will always remember you.
  The nations will praise you for ever and ever.

Psalm 46

*For the director of music. A song of the Sons of Korah.
According to* alamoth.

God is our place of safety. He gives us strength.
  He is always there to help us in times of trouble.
The earth may fall apart.
  The mountains may fall into the middle of the sea.
  But we will not be afraid.
The waters of the sea may roar and foam.
  The mountains may shake when the waters rise.
  But we will not be afraid.

God's blessings are like a river. They fill the city of God
      with joy.
    That city is the holy place where the Most High God
      lives.
Because God is there, the city will not fall.
  God will help it at the beginning of the day.

Nations are in disorder. Kingdoms fall.
God speaks, and the people of the earth melt in fear.

The Lord who rules over all is with us.
The God of Jacob is like a fort to us.

Come and see what the Lord has done.
See the places he has destroyed on the earth.
He makes wars stop from one end of the earth to the
other.
He breaks every bow. He snaps every spear.
He burns every shield with fire.
He says, "Be still, and know that I am God.
I will be honored among the nations.
I will be honored in the earth."

The Lord who rules over all is with us.
The God of Jacob is like a fort to us.

Psalm 47

For the director of music. A psalm of the Sons of Korah.

Clap your hands, all you nations.
Shout to God with cries of joy.
Do this because the Lord Most High is wonderful.
He is the great King over the whole earth.
He brought nations under our control.
He made them fall under us.
He chose our land for us.
The people of Jacob are proud of their land,
and God loves them.

God went up to his throne while his people were shouting
with joy.
The Lord went up while trumpets were playing.
Sing praises to God. Sing praises.
Sing praises to our King. Sing praises.

God is the King of the whole earth.
Sing a psalm of praise to him.

God rules over the nations.

He is seated on his holy throne.

The nobles of the nations come together.

They are now part of the people of the God of Abraham.

The kings of the earth belong to God.

He is greatly honored.

remember what you read

1. What is something you noticed for the first time?

That in church when we sing none of the adults
have any enthusiasm to dance, but in the Bible
they dance and shout their praises to
God and I think we should do that.

2. What questions did you have?

3. Was there anything that bothered you?

4. What did you learn about loving God?

5. What did you learn about loving others?

Psalm 50

A psalm of Asaph.

The Mighty One, God, the Lord, speaks.
  He calls out to the earth
from the sunrise in the east
  to the sunset in the west.
From Zion, perfect and beautiful,
  God's glory shines out.
Our God comes, and he won't be silent.
  A burning fire goes ahead of him.
  A terrible storm is all around him.
He calls out to heaven and earth to be his witnesses.
  Then he judges his people.
He says, "Gather this holy people around me.
  They made a covenant with me by offering a
    sacrifice."
The heavens announce that what God decides is
    right.
  That's because he is a God of justice.

God says, "Listen, my people, and I will speak.
  I will be a witness against you, Israel.
  I am God, your God.
I don't bring charges against you because of your sacrifices.
  I don't bring charges because of the burnt offerings
    you always bring me.
I don't need a bull from your barn.
  I don't need goats from your pens.

Every animal in the forest already belongs to me.
　　And so do the cattle on a thousand hills.
I own every bird in the mountains.
　　The insects in the fields belong to me.
If I were hungry, I wouldn't tell you.
　　The world belongs to me. And so does everything in it.
Do I eat the meat of bulls?
　　Do I drink the blood of goats?
Bring me thank offerings, because I am your God.
　　Carry out the promises you made to me, because I am
　　　　the Most High God.
Call out to me when trouble comes.
　　I will save you. And you will honor me."

But here is what God says to a sinful person.

"What right do you have to speak the words of
　　　　my laws?
How dare you speak the words of my covenant!
You hate my teaching.
　　You turn your back on what I say.
When you see a thief, you join him.
　　You make friends with those who commit adultery.
You use your mouth to speak evil.
　　You use your tongue to spread lies.
You are a witness against your brother.
　　You always tell lies about your own mother's son.
When you did these things, I kept silent.
　　So you thought I was just like you.
But now I'm going to bring you to court.
　　I will bring charges against you.

"You who forget God, think about this.
　　If you don't, I will tear you to pieces.
　　No one will be able to save you.
People who sacrifice thank offerings to me honor me.
　　To those who are without blame I will show my power
　　　　to save."

Psalm 51

*For the director of music. A psalm of David when the prophet
Nathan came to him. Nathan came to him after David
had committed adultery with Bathsheba.*

God, have mercy on me
according to your faithful love.
Because your love is so tender and kind,
wipe out my lawless acts.
Wash away all the evil things I've done.
Make me pure from my sin.

I know the lawless acts I've committed.
I can't forget my sin.
You are the one I've really sinned against.
I've done what is evil in your sight.
So you are right when you sentence me.
You are fair when you judge me.
I know I've been a sinner ever since I was born.
I've been a sinner ever since my mother became pregnant
with me.
I know that you wanted faithfulness even when I was in my
mother's body.
You taught me wisdom in that secret place.

Sprinkle me with hyssop, then I will be clean.
Wash me, then I will be whiter than snow.
Let me hear you say, "Your sins are forgiven."
That will bring me joy and gladness.
Let the body you have broken be glad.
Take away all my sins.
Wipe away all the evil things I've done.

God, create a pure heart in me.
Give me a new spirit that is faithful to you.
Don't send me away from you.
Don't take your Holy Spirit away from me.
Give me back the joy that comes from being saved by you.
Give me a spirit that obeys you so that I will keep going.

Then I will teach your ways to those who commit lawless
    acts.
    And sinners will turn back to you.
You are the God who saves me.
    I have committed murder.
    God, take away my guilt.
Then my tongue will sing about how right you are
    no matter what you do.
Lord, open my lips so that I can speak.
    Then my mouth will praise you.
You don't take delight in sacrifice.
    If you did, I would bring it.
    You don't take pleasure in burnt offerings.
The greatest sacrifice you want is a broken spirit.
    God, you will gladly accept a heart
    that is broken because of sadness over sin.

May you be pleased to give Zion success.
    May it please you to build up the walls of Jerusalem.
Then you will delight in the sacrifices of those who do what
    is right.
    Whole burnt offerings will bring delight to you.
    And bulls will be offered on your altar.

Psalm 53

For the director of music. According to mahalath. *A* maskil *of David.*

Foolish people say in their hearts,
    "There is no God."
They do all kinds of horrible and evil things.
    No one does anything good.

God looks down from heaven
    on all people.
He wants to see if there are any who understand.
    He wants to see if there are any who trust in God.
All of them have turned away.
    They have all become evil.

No one does anything good,
   no one at all.

Don't these people who do evil know anything?
   They eat up my people as if they were eating bread.
   They never call out to God for help.
Just look at them! They are filled with terror
   even when there is nothing to be afraid of!
People of Israel, God scattered the bones of those who
      attacked you.
   You put them to shame, because God hated them.

How I pray that the God who saves Israel will come out of
      Zion!
   God will bless his people with great success again.
   Then let the people of Jacob be filled with joy! Let Israel
      be glad!

Psalm 57

For the director of music. A miktam *of David
when he had run away from Saul into the cave.
To the tune of "Do Not Destroy."*

Have mercy on me, God. Have mercy on me.
   I go to you for safety.
I will find safety in the shadow of your wings.
   There I will stay until the danger is gone.

I cry out to God Most High.
   I cry out to God, and he shows that I am right.
He answers from heaven and saves me.
   He puts to shame those who chase me.
   He shows his love and that he is faithful.

Men who are like lions are all around me.
   I am forced to lie down among people who are like hungry
      animals.
Their teeth are like spears and arrows.
   Their tongues are like sharp swords.

God, may you be honored above the heavens.
Let your glory be over the whole earth.

My enemies spread a net to catch me by the feet.
I felt helpless.
They dug a pit in my path.
But they fell into it themselves.

God, my heart feels secure.
My heart feels secure.
I will sing and make music to you.
My spirit, wake up!
Harp and lyre, wake up!
I want to sing and make music before the sun rises.

Lord, I will praise you among the nations.
I will sing about you among the people of the earth.
Great is your love. It reaches to the heavens.
Your truth reaches to the skies.

God, may you be honored above the heavens.
Let your glory be over the whole earth.

Psalm 61

*For the director of music. A psalm of David to
be played on stringed instruments.*

God, hear my cry for help.
Listen to my prayer.

From a place far away I call out to you.
I call out as my heart gets weaker.
Lead me to the safety of a rock that is high above me.
You have always kept me safe from my enemies.
You are like a strong tower to me.

I long to live in your holy tent forever.
There I find safety in the shadow of your wings.
God, you have heard my promises.
You have given me what belongs to those who worship you.

Add many days to the king's life.
Let him live on and on for many years.
May he always enjoy your blessing as he rules.
Let your love and truth keep him safe.

Then I will always sing praise to you.
I will keep my promises day after day.

remember what you read

1. What is something you noticed for the first time?

That David was a faithful man to God and that even his little sins he asked for foregiveness.

2. What questions did you have?

None

3. Was there anything that bothered you?

No

4. What did you learn about loving God?

That God wants us to ask for foregiveness everytime we sin. He wants us to be clean so that is why we pray to God so that we can have foregiveness.

5. What did you learn about loving others?

That if they have trouble knowing what to pray you could tell them to read the psalms and that they may find something to pray from them

Psalm 63

A psalm of David when he was in the Desert of Judah.

God, you are my God.
  I seek you with all my heart.
With all my strength I thirst for you
  in this dry desert
  where there isn't any water.

Need to do!

I have seen you in the sacred tent.
  There I have seen your power and your glory.
Your love is better than life.
  So I will bring glory to you with my lips.
I will praise you as long as I live.
  I will call on your name when I lift up my hands in
      prayer.
I will be as satisfied as if I had eaten the best food there is.
  I will sing praise to you with my mouth.

As I lie on my bed I remember you.
  I think of you all night long.
Because you have helped me,
  I sing in the shadow of your wings.
I hold on to you tightly.
  Your powerful right hand takes good care of me.

Those who want to kill me will be destroyed.
  They will go down into the grave.
They will be killed by swords.
  They will become food for wild dogs.

But the king will be filled with joy because of what God has
    done.
  All those who make promises in God's name will be able
    to brag.
But the mouths of liars will be shut.

Psalm 64

For the director of music. A psalm of David.

God, hear me as I tell you my problem.
  Don't let my enemies kill me.
Hide me from evil people who talk about how to harm me.
  Hide me from those people who are planning to do evil.

They make their tongues like sharp swords.
  They aim their mean words like deadly arrows.
They shoot from their hiding places at people who aren't
    guilty.
  They shoot quickly and aren't afraid of being caught.

They help one another make evil plans.
  They talk about hiding their traps.
  They say, "Who can see what we are doing?"
They make plans to do what is evil.
  They say, "We have thought up a perfect plan!"
  The hearts and minds of people are so clever!

But God will shoot my enemies with his arrows.
  He will suddenly strike them down.
He will turn their own words against them.
  He will destroy them.
All those who see them will shake their heads
  and look down on them.

All people will respect God.
  They will tell about his works.
  They will think about what he has done.
Godly people will be full of joy because of what the Lord has
    done.

They will go to him for safety.
All those whose hearts are honest will be proud of what he
has done.

Psalm 65

For the director of music. A psalm of David. A song.

Our God, we look forward to praising you in Zion.
We will keep our promises to you.
All people will come to you,
because you hear and answer prayer.
When our sins became too much for us,
you forgave our lawless acts.
Blessed are those you choose
and bring near to worship you.
You bring us into the courtyards of your holy temple.
There in your house we are filled with all kinds of
good things.

God our Savior, you answer us with right and wonderful
deeds.
People all over the world and beyond the farthest oceans
put their hope in you.
You formed the mountains by your power.
You showed how strong you are.
You calmed the oceans and their roaring waves.
You calmed the angry words and actions of the
nations.
Everyone on earth is amazed at the wonderful things
you have done.
What you do makes people from one end of the earth
to the other sing for joy.

You take care of the land and water it.
You make it able to grow many crops.
You fill your streams with water.
You do that to provide the people with grain.
That's what you have decided to do for the land.

You water its rows.
  You smooth out its bumps.
You soften it with showers.
  And you bless its crops.
You bring the year to a close with huge crops.
  You provide more than enough food.
The grass grows thick even in the desert.
  The hills are dressed with gladness.
The meadows are covered with flocks and herds.
  The valleys are dressed with grain.
  They sing and shout for joy.

Psalm 66

For the director of music. A song. A psalm.

Shout to God for joy, everyone on earth!
  Sing about the glory of his name!
  Give him glorious praise!
Say to God, "What wonderful things you do!
  Your power is so great
  that your enemies bow down to you in fear.
Everyone on earth bows down to you.
  They sing praise to you.
  They sing the praises of your name."   *I wish*

Come and see what God has done.
  See what wonderful things he has done for people!
He turned the Red Sea into dry land.
  The people of Israel passed through the waters on foot.
  Come, let us be full of joy because of what he did.
He rules by his power forever.
  His eyes watch the nations.
  Let no one who refuses to obey him rise up against him.

Praise our God, all you nations.
  Let the sound of the praise you give him be heard.
He has kept us alive.
  He has kept our feet from slipping.

God, you have tested us.
    You put us through fire to make us like silver.
You put us in prison.
    You placed heavy loads on our backs.
You let our enemies ride their chariots over our heads.
    We went through fire and water.
But you brought us to a place
    where we have everything we need.

I will come to your temple with burnt offerings.
    I will keep my promises to you.
I made them with my lips.
    My mouth spoke them when I was in trouble.
I will sacrifice fat animals to you as burnt offerings.
    I will offer rams, bulls and goats to you.

Come and hear, all you who have respect for God.
    Let me tell you what he has done for me.
I cried out to him with my mouth.
    I praised him with my tongue.
If I had enjoyed having sin in my heart,
    the Lord would not have listened.
But God has surely listened.
    He has heard my prayer.
Give praise to God.
    He has accepted my prayer.
    He has not held back his love from me.

Psalm 67

*For the director of music. A psalm. A song to be played
on stringed instruments.*

God, have mercy on us and bless us.
    May you be pleased with us.
Then your ways will be known on earth.
    All nations will see that you have the power to save.

God, may the nations praise you.
    May all the people on earth praise you.

May the nations be glad and sing for joy.
   You rule the people of the earth fairly.
   You guide the nations of the earth.
God, may the nations praise you.
   May all the people on earth praise you.

The land produces its crops.
   God, our God, blesses us.
May God continue to bless us.
   Then people from one end of the earth to the other
   will have respect for him.

Psalm 70

For the director of music. A prayer of David.

God, hurry and save me.
   Lord, come quickly and help me.
Let those who are trying to kill me be put to shame.
   Let them not be honored.
Let all those who want to destroy me
   be turned back in shame.
Some people make fun of me.
   Let them be turned back when their plans fail.
But let all those who seek you
   be joyful and glad because of what you have done.
Let those who want you to save them always say,
   "The Lord is great!"

But I am poor and needy.
   God, come quickly to me.
You are the God who helps me and saves me.
   Lord, please don't wait any longer.

remember what you read

1. What is something you noticed for the first time?

That God is great.

2. What questions did you have?

None.

3. Was there anything that bothered you?

No.

4. What did you learn about loving God?

That God doesn't want us to have Joy in things here on earth. He wants us to hae Joy in him.

5. What did you learn about loving others?

In Psalm 65 it says that God answers us right so we can say that to someone if they feel like God won't answer them.

Psalm 73

A psalm of Asaph.

God is truly good to Israel.
    He is good to those who have pure hearts.

But my feet had almost slipped.
    I had almost tripped and fallen.
I saw that proud and sinful people were doing well.
    And I began to long for what they had.

They don't have any troubles.
    Their bodies are healthy and strong.
They don't have the problems most people have.
    They don't suffer as other people do.
Their pride is like a necklace.
    They put on meanness as if it were their clothes.
Many sins come out of their hard and stubborn
        hearts.
    There is no limit to the evil things they can think up.
They laugh at others and speak words of hatred.
    They are proud. They warn others about the harm
        they can do to them.
They brag as if they owned heaven itself.
    They talk as if they controlled the earth.
So people listen to them.
    They lap up their words like water.
They say, "How would God know what we're doing?
    Does the Most High God know anything?"

Here is what sinful people are like.
They don't have a care in the world.
They keep getting richer and richer.

It seems as if I have kept my heart pure for no reason.
It didn't do me any good to wash my hands
to show that I wasn't guilty of doing anything wrong.
Day after day I've been in pain.
God has punished me in a new way every morning.

What if I had talked like that?
Then I wouldn't have been faithful to God's children.
I tried to understand it all.
But it was more than I could handle.
It troubled me until I entered God's temple.
Then I understood what will finally happen to bad people.

God, I'm sure you will make them slip and fall.
You will throw them down and destroy them.
It will happen very suddenly.
A terrible death will take them away completely.
A dream goes away when a person wakes up.
Lord, it will be like that when you rise up.
It will be as if those people were only a dream.

At one time my heart was sad
and my spirit was bitter.
I didn't have any sense. I didn't know anything.
I acted like a wild animal toward you.

But I am always with you.
You hold me by my right hand.
You give me wise advice to guide me.
And when I die, you will take me away
into the glory of heaven.
I don't have anyone in heaven but you.
I don't want anything on earth besides you.
My body and my heart may grow weak.
God, you give strength to my heart.
You are everything I will ever need.

Those who don't want anything to do with you will die.
 You destroy all those who aren't faithful to you.
But I am close to you. And that's good.
 Lord and King, I have made you my place of safety.
 I will talk about everything you have done.

Psalm 75

For the director of music. A psalm of Asaph.
A song to the tune of "Do Not Destroy."

God, we praise you.
 We praise you because you are near to us.
 People talk about the wonderful things you have
   done.

You say, "I choose the appointed time to judge people.
 And I judge them fairly.
When the earth and all its people tremble,
 I keep everything from falling to pieces.
To the proud I say, 'Don't brag anymore.'
 To sinners I say, 'Don't show off your power.
Don't show it off against me.
 Don't talk back to me.' "

No one from east or west or north or south
 can judge themselves.
God is the one who judges.
 He says to one person, "You are guilty."
 To another he says, "You are not guilty."
In the hand of the Lord is a cup.
 It is full of wine mixed with spices.
 It is the wine of his anger.
He pours it out. All the evil people on earth
 drink it down to the very last drop.

I will speak about this forever.
 I will sing praise to the God of Jacob.
God says, "I will destroy the power of all sinful people.
 But I will make godly people more powerful."

Psalm 76

For the director of music. A psalm of Asaph.
A song to be played on stringed instruments.

In the land of Judah, God is well known.
In Israel, his name is great.
His tent is in Jerusalem.
The place where he lives is on Mount Zion.
There he broke the deadly arrows of his enemies.
He broke their shields and swords.
He broke their weapons of war.

God, you shine like a very bright light.
You are more majestic than mountains full of
wild animals.
Brave soldiers have been robbed of everything
they had.
Now they lie there, sleeping in death.
Not one of them can even lift his hands.
God of Jacob, at your command
both horse and chariot lie still.
People should have respect for you alone.
Who can stand in front of you when you are
angry?
From heaven you handed down your sentence.
The land was afraid and became quiet.
God, that happened when you rose up to judge.
It happened when you came to save all your suffering
people in the land.
Your anger against sinners brings you praise.
Those who live through your anger gather to worship
you.

Make promises to the Lord your God and keep them.
Let all the neighboring nations
bring gifts to the God who should be respected.
He breaks the proud spirit of rulers.
The kings of the earth have respect for him.

Psalm 80

For the director of music. A psalm of Asaph to the
tune of "The Lilies of the Covenant."

Shepherd of Israel, hear us.
　　You lead the people of Joseph like a flock.
　　You sit on your throne between the cherubim.
Show your glory
　　to the people of Ephraim, Benjamin and Manasseh.
Call your strength into action.
　　Come and save us.

God, make us new again.
　　May you be pleased with us.
　　Then we will be saved.

Lord God, you rule over all.
　　How long will you be angry?
　　Will you be angry with your people even when they pray to
　　　　you?
You have given us tears as our food.
　　You have made us drink tears by the bowlful.
You have let our neighbors mock us.
　　Our enemies laugh at us.

God who rules over all, make us new again.
　　May you be pleased with us.
　　Then we will be saved.

You brought Israel out of Egypt.
　　Israel was like a vine.
After you drove the nations out of Canaan,
　　you planted the vine in their land.
You prepared the ground for it.
　　It took root and spread out over the whole land.
The mountains were covered with its shade.
　　The shade of its branches covered the mighty cedar trees.
Your vine sent its branches out all the way to the
　　　　Mediterranean Sea.
　　They reached as far as the Euphrates River.

Why have you broken down the walls around your vine?
  Now all who pass by it can pick its grapes.
Wild pigs from the forest destroy it.
  Insects from the fields feed on it.
God who rules over all, return to us!
  Look down from heaven and see us!
Watch over your vine.
  Guard the root you have planted with your powerful right
    hand.
  Take care of the branch you have raised up for yourself.

Your vine has been cut down and burned in the fire.
  You have been angry with us, and we are dying.
May you honor the people at your right hand.
  May you honor the nation you have raised up for yourself.
Then we won't turn away from you.
  Give us new life. We will worship you.

LORD God who rules over all, make us new again.
  May you be pleased with us.
  Then we will be saved.

Psalm 82

A psalm of Asaph.

God takes his place at the head of a large gathering of leaders.
  He announces his decisions among them.

He says, "How long will you stand up for those who aren't
    fair to others?
  How long will you show mercy to sinful people?
Stand up for the weak and for children whose fathers have
    died.
  Protect the rights of people who are poor or treated badly.
Save those who are weak and needy.
  Save them from the power of sinful people.

"You leaders don't know anything.
  You don't understand anything.

You are in the dark about what is right.
　　Law and order have been destroyed all over the world.

"I said, 'You leaders are like gods.
　　You are all children of the Most High God.'
But you will die, like mere human beings.
　　You will die like every other leader."

God, rise up. Judge the earth.
　　All the nations belong to you.

remember what you read

1. What is something you noticed for the first time?

That God wants us to tell everyone about what he did for us.

2. What questions did you have?

None

3. Was there anything that bothered you?

No

4. What did you learn about loving God?

That we shouldn't stand up for things or people that are against God.

5. What did you learn about loving others?

PSALMS, PART 8

Psalm 83

A song. A psalm of Asaph.

God, don't remain silent.
  Don't refuse to listen.
  Do something, God.
See how your enemies are growling like dogs.
  See how they are rising up against you.
They make clever plans against your people.
  They make evil plans against those you love.
"Come," they say. "Let's destroy that whole nation.
  Then the name of Israel won't be remembered
    anymore."

All of them agree on the evil plans they have made.
  They join forces against you.
Their forces include the people of Edom,
  Ishmael, Moab and Hagar.
They also include the people of Byblos, Ammon,
    Amalek,
  Philistia and Tyre.
Even Assyria has joined them
  to give strength to the people of Moab and Ammon.

Do to them what you did to the people of Midian.
  Do to them what you did to Sisera and Jabin at the
    Kishon River.
Sisera and Jabin died near the town of Endor.
  Their bodies were left on the ground like human waste.

Do to the nobles of your enemies what you did to Oreb
    and Zeeb.
    Do to all their princes what you did to Zebah and
        Zalmunna.
They said, "Let's take over
    the grasslands that belong to God."

My God, make them like straw that the wind blows away.
    Make them like tumbleweed.
Destroy them as fire burns up a forest.
    Destroy them as a flame sets mountains on fire.
Chase them with your mighty winds.
    Terrify them with your storm.
Lord, put them to shame
    so that they will seek you.

May they always be filled with terror and shame.
    May they die in dishonor.
May you, the Lord, let your enemies know who you are.
    You alone are the Most High God over the whole earth.

Psalm 84

For the director of music. According to gittith.
A psalm of the Sons of Korah.

Lord who rules over all,
    how lovely is the place where you live!
I can't wait to be in the courtyards of the Lord's temple.
    I really want to be there.
My whole being cries out
    for the living God.

Lord who rules over all,
    even the sparrow has found a home near your altar.
My King and my God,
    the swallow also has a nest there,
    where she may have her young.
Blessed are those who live in your house.
    They are always praising you.

Blessed are those whose strength comes from you.
     They have firmly decided to travel to your temple.
As they pass through the dry Valley of Baka,
     they make it a place where water flows.
     The rain in the fall covers it with pools.
Those people get stronger as they go along,
     until each of them appears in Zion, where God lives.

Lord God who rules over all, hear my prayer.
     God of the people of Jacob, listen to me.
God, may you be pleased with your anointed king.
     You appointed him to be like a shield that keeps
          us safe.

A single day in your courtyards is better
     than a thousand anywhere else.
I would rather guard the door of the house of my God
     than live in the tents of sinful people.
The Lord God is like the sun that gives us light.
     He is like a shield that keeps us safe.
     The Lord blesses us with favor and honor.
He doesn't hold back anything good
     from those whose lives are without blame.

Lord who rules over all,
     blessed is the person who trusts in you.

Psalm 86

A prayer of David.

Lord, hear me and answer me.
     I am poor and needy.
Keep my life safe, because I am faithful to you.
     Save me, because I trust in you.
     You are my God.
Lord, have mercy on me.
     I call out to you all day long.
Bring joy to me.
     Lord, I put my trust in you.

Lord, you are forgiving and good.
　You are full of love for all who call out to you.
Lord, hear my prayer.
　Listen to my cry for mercy.
When I'm in trouble, I will call out to you.
　And you will answer me.

Lord, there's no one like you among the gods.
　No one can do what you do.
Lord, all the nations you have made
　will come and worship you.
　They will bring glory to you.
You are great. You do wonderful things.
　You alone are God.

Lord, teach me how you want me to live.
　Do this so that I will depend on you, my faithful God.
Give me a heart that doesn't want anything
　more than to worship you.
Lord my God, I will praise you with all my heart.
　I will bring glory to you forever.
Great is your love for me.
　You have kept me from going down into the place of the
　　dead.

God, proud people are attacking me.
　A gang of mean people is trying to kill me.
　They don't care about you.
But Lord, you are a God who is tender and kind.
　You are gracious.
You are slow to get angry.
　You are faithful and full of love.
Come to my aid and have mercy on me.
　Show your strength by helping me.
　Save me because I serve you just as my mother did.
Prove your goodness to me.
　Then my enemies will see it and be put to shame.
　Lord, you have helped me and given me comfort.

Psalm 87

A psalm of the Sons of Korah. A song.

The LORD has built his city
    on the holy mountain.
He loves the city of Zion
    more than all the other places
    where the people of Jacob live.
City of God,
    the LORD says glorious things about you.
He says, "I will include Egypt and Babylon
    in a list of nations who recognize me as king.
I will also include Philistia and Tyre, along with Cush.
    I will say about them, 'They were born in Zion.'"

Certainly it will be said about Zion,
    "This nation and that nation were born in it.
    The Most High God himself will make it secure."
Here is what the LORD will write in his list of the nations.
    "Each of them was born in Zion."
As they make music they will sing,
    "Zion, all our blessings come from you."

Psalm 88

For the director of music. According to mahalath leannoth. *A song.*
A psalm of the Sons of Korah. A maskil *of Heman the Ezrahite.*

LORD, you are the God who saves me.
    Day and night I cry out to you.
Please hear my prayer.
    Pay attention to my cry for help.

I have so many troubles
    I'm about to die.
People think my life is over.
    I'm like someone who doesn't have any strength.
People treat me as if I were dead.
    I'm like those who have been killed and are now in the
        grave.

You don't even remember them anymore.
>They are cut off from your care.

It's as if you have put me deep down in the grave.
>It's as if you have put me in that deep, dark place.

Your great anger lies heavy on me.
>All the waves of your anger have crashed over me.

You have taken my closest friends away from me.
>You have made me sickening to them.

I feel trapped and can't escape.
>I'm crying so much I can't see very well.

Lord, I call out to you every day.
>I lift up my hands to you in prayer.

Do you do wonderful things for those who are dead?
>Do their spirits rise up and praise you?

Do those who are dead speak about your love?
>Do those who are in the grave tell how faithful you are?

Are your wonderful deeds known in that dark place?
>Are your holy acts known in that land where the dead are
>forgotten?

Lord, I cry out to you for help.
>In the morning I pray to you.

Lord, why do you say no to me?
>Why do you turn your face away from me?

I've been in pain ever since I was young.
>I've been close to death.

You have made me suffer terrible things.
>I have lost all hope.

Your great anger has swept over me.
>Your terrors have destroyed me.

All day long they surround me like a flood.
>They have closed in all around me.

You have taken my friends and neighbors away from me.
>Darkness is my closest friend.

remember what you read

1. What is something you noticed for the first time?

That the Psalms kind of give you words to pray.

2. What questions did you have?

None.

3. Was there anything that bothered you?

No.

4. What did you learn about loving God?

That God is slow to get angery and punishes us so that we will then seek him.

5. What did you learn about loving others?

That we need to pray to God for other people because they may be in danger or in need of God.

Sing a new song

Psalm 91

Whoever rests in the shadow of the Most High God
  will be kept safe by the Mighty One.
I will say about the LORD,
  "He is my place of safety.
He is like a fort to me.
  He is my God. I trust in him."

He will certainly save you from hidden traps
  and from deadly sickness.
He will cover you with his wings.
  Under the feathers of his wings you will find
    safety.
  He is faithful. He will keep you safe like a shield
    or a tower.
You won't have to be afraid of the terrors that come
    during the night.
  You won't have to fear the arrows that come at you
    during the day.
You won't have to be afraid of the sickness that attacks
    in the darkness.
  You won't have to fear the plague that destroys at
    noon.
A thousand may fall dead at your side.
  Ten thousand may fall near your right hand.
  But no harm will come to you.
You will see with your own eyes
  how God punishes sinful people.

Suppose you say, "The LORD is the one who keeps me safe."
  Suppose you let the Most High God be like a home to you.
Then no harm will come to you.
  No terrible plague will come near your tent.
The LORD will command his angels
  to take good care of you.
They will lift you up in their hands.
  Then you won't trip over a stone.
You will walk on lions and cobras.
  You will crush mighty lions and poisonous snakes.

The LORD says, "I will save the one who loves me.
  I will keep him safe, because he trusts in me.
He will call out to me, and I will answer him.
  I will be with him in times of trouble.
  I will save him and honor him.
I will give him a long and full life.
  I will save him."

Psalm 93

The LORD rules.
  He puts on majesty as if it were clothes.
  The LORD puts on majesty and strength.
Indeed, the world has been set in place.
  It is firm and secure.
LORD, you began to rule a long time ago.
  You have always existed.

LORD, the seas have lifted up their voice.
  They have lifted up their pounding waves.
But LORD, you are more powerful than the roar of the
      ocean.
  You are stronger than the waves of the sea.
  LORD, you are powerful in heaven.

Your laws do not change, LORD.
  Your temple will be holy
  for all time to come.

Psalm 98

A psalm.

Sing a new song to the LORD.
  He has done wonderful things.
By the power of his right hand and his holy arm
  he has saved his people.
The LORD has made known his power to save.
  He has shown the nations that he does what is right.
He has shown his faithful love
  to the people of Israel.
People from one end of the earth to the other
  have seen that our God has saved us.

Shout for joy to the LORD, everyone on earth.
  Burst into joyful songs and make music.
Make music to the LORD with the harp.
  Sing and make music with the harp.
Blow the trumpets. Give a blast on the ram's horn.
  Shout for joy to the LORD. He is the King.

Let the ocean and everything in it roar.
  Let the world and all who live in it shout.
Let the rivers clap their hands.
  Let the mountains sing together with joy.
Let them sing to the LORD,
  because he is coming to judge the earth.
He will judge the nations of the world
  in keeping with what is right and fair.

Psalm 100

A psalm for giving grateful praise.

Shout for joy to the LORD, everyone on earth.
  Worship the LORD with gladness.
  Come to him with songs of joy.
Know that the LORD is God.
  He made us, and we belong to him.

We are his people.
   We are the sheep belonging to his flock.

Give thanks as you enter the gates of his temple.
   Give praise as you enter its courtyards.
   Give thanks to him and praise his name.
The Lord is good. His faithful love continues forever.
   It will last for all time to come.

Psalm 105

Give praise to the Lord and announce who he is.
   Tell the nations what he has done.
Sing to him, sing praise to him.
   Tell about all the wonderful things he has done.
Praise him, because his name is holy.
   Let the hearts of those who trust in the Lord be glad.
Seek the Lord and the strength he gives.
   Always seek him.

Remember the wonderful things he has done.
   Remember his miracles and how he judged our enemies.
Remember what he has done, you children of his servant
      Abraham.
   Remember it, you people of Jacob, God's chosen ones.
He is the Lord our God.
   He judges the whole earth.

He will keep his covenant forever.
   He will keep his promise for all time to come.
He will keep the covenant he made with Abraham.
   He will keep the promise he made to Isaac.
He made it stand as a law for Jacob.
   He made it stand as a covenant for Israel that will last
      forever.
He said, "I will give you the land of Canaan.
   It will belong to you."

At first there weren't very many of God's people.
   There were only a few, and they were strangers in the land.

They wandered from nation to nation.
>They wandered from one kingdom to another.
But God didn't allow anyone to treat them badly.
>To keep them safe, he gave a command to kings.
He said to them, "Do not touch my anointed ones.
>Do not harm my prophets."

He made the people in the land go hungry.
>He destroyed all their food supplies.
He sent a man ahead of them into Egypt.
>That man was Joseph. He had been sold as a slave.
The Egyptians put his feet in chains.
>They put an iron collar around his neck.
He was in prison until what he said would happen came true.
>The word of the LORD proved that he was right.
The king of Egypt sent for Joseph and let him out of prison.
>The ruler of many nations set him free.
He put Joseph in charge of his palace.
>He made him ruler over everything he owned.
Joseph was in charge of teaching the princes.
>He taught the elders how to think and live wisely.

Then the rest of Jacob's family went to Egypt.
>The people of Israel lived as outsiders in the land of Ham.
The LORD gave his people so many children
>that there were too many of them for their enemies.
He made the Egyptians hate his people.
>The Egyptians made evil plans against them.
The LORD sent his servant Moses to the king of Egypt.
>He sent Aaron, his chosen one, along with him.
The LORD gave them the power to do signs among the
>Egyptians.
>They did his wonders in the land of Ham.
The LORD sent darkness over the land.
>He did it because the Egyptians had refused to obey his
>words.
He turned their rivers and streams into blood.
>He caused the fish in them to die.

Their land was covered with frogs.
  Frogs even went into the bedrooms of the rulers.
The Lord spoke, and large numbers of flies came.
  Gnats filled the whole country.
He turned their rain into hail.
  Lightning flashed all through their land.
He destroyed their vines and fig trees.
  He broke down the trees in Egypt.
He spoke, and the locusts came.
  There were so many of them they couldn't be counted.
They ate up every green thing in the land.
  They ate up what the land produced.
Then he killed the oldest son of every family in Egypt.
  He struck down the oldest of all their sons.

He brought the people of Israel out of Egypt.
  The Egyptians loaded them down with silver and gold.
  From among the tribes of Israel no one got tired or fell
    down.
The Egyptians were glad when the people of Israel left.
  They were terrified because of Israel.
The Lord spread out a cloud to cover his people.
  He gave them a fire to light up the night.
They asked for meat, and he brought them quail.
  He fed them well with manna, the bread of heaven.
He broke open a rock, and streams of water poured out.
  They flowed like a river in the desert.

He remembered the holy promise
  he had made to his servant Abraham.
His chosen people shouted for joy
  as he brought them out of Egypt.
He gave them the lands of other nations.
  He let them take over what others had worked for.
He did it so they might obey his rules
  and follow his laws.

Praise the Lord.

remember what you read

1. What is something you noticed for the first time?

That back then people had to tell
one another because back then not
everyone could read.

2. What questions did you have?

None

3. Was there anything that bothered you?

No

4. What did you learn about loving God?

That we should be praising God
by shouting dancing really into it.

5. What did you learn about loving others?

We can say to them if they are
new that the be king and fit
in even if they don't feel like
it.

PSALMS, PART 10

Psalm 110

A psalm of David.

The Lord says to my lord,
  "Sit at my right hand
until I put your enemies
  under your control."

The Lord will make your royal authority spread out from
      Zion to other lands.
  He says, "Rule over your enemies who are all around you."
Your troops will be willing to fight for you
  on the day of battle.
Your young men will be wrapped in holy majesty.
  They will come to you like the fresh dew that falls early in
    the morning.

The Lord has made a promise.
  He will not change his mind.
He has said, "You are a priest forever,
  just like Melchizedek."

The Lord is at your right hand.
  He will crush kings on the day when he is angry.
He will judge the nations. He will pile up dead bodies on the
    field of battle.
  He will crush the rulers of the whole earth.
He will drink from a brook along the way and receive new
    strength.
  And so he will win the battle.

Psalm 111

Praise the LORD.

I will praise the LORD with all my heart.
  I will praise him where honest people gather for worship.

The LORD has done great things.
  All who take delight in those things think deeply about
    them.
What he does shows his glory and majesty.
  He will always do what is right.
The LORD causes his wonders to be remembered.
  He is kind and tender.
He provides food for those who have respect for him.
  He remembers his covenant forever.
He has shown his people what his power can do.
  He has given them the lands of other nations.
He is faithful and right in everything he does.
  All his rules can be trusted.
They will stand firm for ever and ever.
  They were given by the LORD.
  He is faithful and honest.
He set his people free.
  He made a covenant with them that will last forever.
  His name is holy and wonderful.

If you really want to become wise,
  you must begin by having respect for the LORD.
All those who follow his rules have good understanding.
  People should praise him forever.

Psalm 112

Praise the LORD.

Blessed are those who have respect for the LORD.
  They find great delight when they obey God's commands.

Their children will be powerful in the land.
  Because they are honest, their children will be blessed.

Their family will have wealth and riches.
  They will always be blessed for doing what is right.
Even in the darkness light shines on honest people.
  It shines on those who are kind and tender and godly.
Good things will come to those who are willing to lend
      freely.
  Good things will come to those who are fair in everything
      they do.
Those who do what is right will always be secure.
  They will be remembered forever.
They aren't afraid when bad news comes.
  They stand firm because they trust in the LORD.
Their hearts are secure. They aren't afraid.
  In the end they will see their enemies destroyed.
They have spread their gifts around to poor people.
  Their good works continue forever.
  They will be powerful and honored.

Evil people will see it and be upset.
  They will grind their teeth and become weaker and weaker.
  What evil people long to do can't succeed.

Psalm 113

Praise the LORD.

Praise him, you who serve the LORD.
  Praise the name of the LORD.
Let us praise the name of the LORD,
  both now and forever.
From the sunrise in the east to the sunset in the west,
  may the name of the LORD be praised.

The LORD is honored over all the nations. I wish
  His glory reaches to the highest heavens.
Who is like the LORD our God?
  He sits on his throne in heaven.
He bends down to look
  at the heavens and the earth.

He raises poor people up from the trash pile.
　　He lifts needy people out of the ashes.
He causes them to sit with princes.
　　He causes them to sit with the princes of his people.
He gives children to the woman who doesn't have any children.
　　He makes her a happy mother in her own home.

Praise the Lord.

Psalm 115

Lord, may glory be given to you, not to us.
　　You are loving and faithful.

Why do the nations ask,
　　"Where is their God?"
Our God is in heaven.
　　He does anything he wants to do.
But the statues of their gods are made out of silver and gold.
　　They are made by human hands.
They have mouths but can't speak.
　　They have eyes but can't see.
They have ears but can't hear.
　　They have noses but can't smell.
They have hands but can't feel.
　　They have feet but can't walk.
　　They have throats but can't say anything.
Those who make statues of gods will be like them.
　　So will all those who trust in them.

All you Israelites, trust in the Lord.
　　He helps you like a shield that keeps you safe.
Priests of Aaron, trust in the Lord.
　　He helps you like a shield that keeps you safe.
You who have respect for the Lord, trust in him.
　　He helps you like a shield that keeps you safe.

The Lord remembers us and will bless us.
　　He will bless Israel, his people.
　　He will bless the priests of Aaron.

The Lord will bless those who have respect for him.
   He will bless important and unimportant people alike.

May the Lord give you many children.
   May he give them to you and to your children after you.
May the Lord bless you.
   He is the Maker of heaven and earth.

The highest heavens belong to the Lord.
   But he has given the earth to human beings.
Dead people don't praise the Lord.
   Those who lie quietly in the grave don't praise him.
But we who are alive praise the Lord,
   both now and forever.

Praise the Lord.

Psalm 116

I love the Lord, because he heard my voice.
   He heard my cry for his help.
Because he paid attention to me,
   I will call out to him as long as I live.

The ropes of death were wrapped around me.
   The horrors of the grave came over me.
   I was overcome by sadness and sorrow.
Then I called out to the Lord.
   I cried out, "Lord, save me!"

The Lord is holy and kind.
   Our God is full of tender love.
The Lord takes care of those who are not aware of danger.
   When I was in great need, he saved me.

I said to myself, "Be calm.
   The Lord has been good to me."

Lord, you have saved me from death.
   You have dried the tears from my eyes.
   You have kept me from tripping and falling.

So now I can enjoy life here with you
   while I'm still living.
I trusted in the LORD even when I said to myself,
   "I am in great pain."
When I was terrified, I said to myself,
   "No one tells the truth."

The LORD has been so good to me!
   How can I ever pay him back?
I will bring an offering of wine to the LORD
   and thank him for saving me.
   I will worship him.
In front of all the LORD's people,
   I will do what I promised him.

The LORD pays special attention
   when his faithful people die.
LORD, I serve you.
   I serve you just as my mother did.
   You have set me free from the chains of my suffering.

LORD, I will sacrifice a thank offering to you.
   I will worship you.
In front of all the LORD's people,
   I will do what I promised him.
I will keep my promise in the courtyards of the LORD's
     temple.
   I will keep my promise in Jerusalem itself.

Praise the LORD.

Psalm 117

All you nations, praise the LORD.
   All you people on earth, praise him.
Great is his love for us.
   The LORD is faithful forever.

Praise the LORD.

remember what you read

1. What is something you noticed for the first time?

That God is good and wonderful
so we should praise him all the time.

2. What questions did you have?

None

3. Was there anything that bothered you?

No

4. What did you learn about loving God?

That God is a faithful God and we aren't
always faithful to Him like we should
be.

5. What did you learn about loving others?

That we can use Psalm 115 if they
feel like God hasn't remembered them.

Psalm 119

*[This psalm praises God for his law. Each part starts
with a letter from the Hebrew alphabet. Every
other line you see here starts with the same letter
in Hebrew. This is called an "acrostic poem."]*

א Aleph

Blessed are those who live without blame.
    They live in keeping with the law of the Lord.
Blessed are those who obey his covenant laws.
    They trust in him with all their hearts.
They don't do anything wrong.
    They live as he wants them to live.
You have given me rules
    that I must obey completely.
I hope I will always stand firm
    in following your orders.
Then I won't be put to shame
    when I think about all your commands.
I will praise you with an honest heart
    as I learn about how fair your decisions are.
I will obey your orders.
    Please don't leave me all alone.

ב Beth

How can a young person keep their life pure?
    By living according to your word.
I trust in you with all my heart.
    Don't let me wander away from your commands.

I have hidden your word in my heart
  so that I won't sin against you.
LORD, I give praise to you.
  Teach me your orders.
With my lips I talk about
  all the decisions you have made.
Following your covenant laws gives me joy
  just as great riches give joy to others.
I spend time thinking about your rules.
  I consider how you want me to live.
I take delight in your orders.
  I won't fail to obey your word.

ג Gimel

Be good to me while I am alive.
  Do this so that I may obey your word.
Open my eyes so that I can see
  the wonderful truths in your law.
I'm a stranger on earth.
  Don't hide your commands from me.
My heart is filled with longing
  for your laws at all times.
You correct proud people. They are under your curse.
  They wander away from your commands.
I obey your covenant laws.
  So don't let evil people laugh at me or hate me.
Even if rulers sit together and tell lies about me,
  I will spend time thinking about your orders.
Your covenant laws are my delight.
  They give me wise advice.

ו Waw

LORD, show me your faithful love.
  Save me as you have promised.
Then I can answer anyone who makes fun of me,
  because I trust in your word.
Help me always to tell the truth about how faithful you are.
  I have put my hope in your laws.

I will always obey your law,
for ever and ever.
I will lead a full and happy life,
because I've tried to obey your rules.
I will talk about your covenant laws to kings.
I will not be put to shame.
I take delight in obeying your commands
because I love them.
I reach out for your commands that I love.
I do this so that I may think deeply about your orders.

ז Zayin

Remember what you have said to me.
You have given me hope.
Even when I suffer, I am comforted
because you promised to keep me alive.
Proud people make fun of me without mercy.
But I don't turn away from your law.
Lord, I remember the laws you gave long ago.
I find comfort in them.
I am very angry
because evil people have turned away from your law.
No matter where I live,
I sing about your orders.
Lord, during the night I remember who you are.
That's why I keep your law.
I have really done my best
to obey your rules.

ט Teth

Lord, be good to me
as you have promised.
Increase my knowledge and give me good sense,
because I trust your commands.
Before I went through suffering, I went down the wrong path.
But now I obey your word.
You are good, and what you do is good.
Teach me your orders.

The lies of proud people have taken away my good name.
  But I follow your rules with all my heart.
Their unfeeling hearts are hard and stubborn.
  But I take delight in your law.
It was good for me to suffer.
  That's what helped me to understand your orders.
The law you gave is worth more to me
  than thousands of pieces of silver and gold.

י Yodh

You made me and formed me with your own hands.
  Give me understanding so that I can learn your
    commands.
May those who have respect for you be filled with joy
    when they see me.
  I have put my hope in your word.
Lord, I know that your laws are right.
  You were faithful to your promise when you made me
    suffer.
May your faithful love comfort me
  as you have promised me.
Show me your tender love so that I can live.
  I take delight in your law.
May proud people be put to shame for treating me badly for
    no reason.
  I will think deeply about your rules.
May those who have respect for you come to me.
  Then I can teach them your covenant laws.
May I follow your orders with all my heart.
  Then I won't be put to shame.

נ Nun

Your word is like a lamp that shows me the way.
  It is like a light that guides me.
I have made a promise
  to follow your laws, because they are right.
I have suffered very much.
  Lord, keep me alive as you have promised.

Lord, accept the praise I freely give you.
  Teach me your laws.
I keep putting my life in danger.
  But I won't forget to obey your law.
Evil people have set a trap for me.
  But I haven't wandered away from your rules.
Your covenant laws are your gift to me forever.
  They fill my heart with joy.
I have decided to obey your orders
  to the very end.

פ Pe

Your covenant laws are wonderful.
  So I obey them.
When your words are made clear, they bring light.
  They bring understanding to childish people.
I open my mouth and pant like a dog,
  because I long to know your commands.
Turn to me and have mercy on me.
  That's what you've always done for those who love you.
Teach me how to live as you have promised.
  Don't let any sin be my master.
Set me free from people who treat me badly.
  Then I will obey your rules.
Have mercy on me.
  Teach me your orders.
Streams of tears flow from my eyes,
  because people don't obey your law.

ת Taw

Lord, may you hear my cry.
  Give me understanding, just as you said you would.
May you hear my prayer.
  Save me, just as you promised.
May my lips pour out praise to you,
  because you teach me your orders.
May my tongue sing about your word,
  because all your commands are right.

May your hand be ready to help me,
  because I have chosen to obey your rules.
Lord, I long for you to save me.
  Your law gives me delight.
Let me live so that I can praise you.
  May your laws keep me going.
Like a lost sheep, I've gone down the wrong path.
  Come and look for me,
  because I haven't forgotten to obey your commands.

remember what you read

1. What is something you noticed for the first time?

When David wrote this he remembered
all the promises that God said to him.

2. What questions did you have?

None

3. Was there anything that bothered you?

No

4. What did you learn about loving God?

That if we don't ask God to open
our mind when we read the Bible
then we won't learn anything.

5. What did you learn about loving others?

That if we see somebody and they think
they are ugly we can use the verse in
Psalm 119 to comfort them and that they
know that they look perfect because
God love them's
and formed them.

Give thanks to the Lord

Psalm 121

A song for those who go up to Jerusalem to worship the LORD.

I look up to the mountains.
  Where does my help come from?
My help comes from the LORD.
  He is the Maker of heaven and earth.

He won't let your foot slip.
  He who watches over you won't get tired.
In fact, he who watches over Israel
  won't get tired or go to sleep.

The LORD watches over you.
  The LORD is like a shade tree at your right hand.
The sun won't harm you during the day.
  The moon won't harm you during the night.

The LORD will keep you from every kind of harm.
  He will watch over your life.
The LORD will watch over your life no matter where you go,
  both now and forever.

Psalm 122

*A song for those who go up to Jerusalem to worship
the LORD. A psalm of David.*

I was very glad when they said to me,
  "Let us go up to the house of the LORD."
Jerusalem, our feet are standing
  inside your gates.

Jerusalem is built like a city
    where everything is close together.
The tribes of the LORD go there to praise his name.
    They do it in keeping with the law he gave to Israel.
The thrones of the family line of David are there.
    That's where the people are judged.

Pray for the peace of Jerusalem. Say,
    "May those who love you be secure.
May there be peace inside your walls.
    May your people be kept safe."
I'm concerned for my family and friends.
    So I say to Jerusalem, "May you enjoy peace."
I'm concerned about the house of the LORD our God.
    So I pray that things will go well with Jerusalem.

Psalm 127

*A song for those who go up to Jerusalem to worship
the LORD. A psalm of Solomon.*

If the LORD doesn't build a house,
    the work of the builders is useless.
If the LORD doesn't watch over a city,
    it's useless for those on guard duty to stand watch
        over it.
It's useless for you to work from early morning
    until late at night
just to get food to eat.
    God provides for those he loves even while they sleep.

Children are a gift from the LORD.
    They are a reward from him.
Children who are born to people when they are young
    are like arrows in the hands of a soldier.
Blessed are those
    who have many children.
They won't be put to shame
    when they go up against their enemies in court.

Psalm 130

A song for those who go up to Jerusalem to worship the LORD.

LORD, I cry out to you
  because I'm suffering so deeply.
Lord, listen to me.
  Pay attention to my cry for your mercy.

LORD, suppose you kept a close watch on sins.
  Lord, who then wouldn't be found guilty?
But you forgive.
  So we can serve you with respect.

With all my heart I wait for the LORD to help me.
  I put my hope in his word.
I wait for the Lord to help me.
  I want his help more than night watchmen want the
    morning to come.
I'll say it again.
  I want his help more than night watchmen want the
    morning to come.
Israel, put your hope in the LORD,
  because the LORD's love never fails.
  He sets his people completely free.
He himself will set Israel
  free from all their sins.

Psalm 131

*A song for those who go up to Jerusalem to worship
the LORD. A psalm of David.*

LORD, my heart isn't proud.
  My eyes aren't proud either.
I don't concern myself with important matters.
  I don't concern myself with things that are too wonderful
    for me.
I have made myself calm and content
  like a young child in its mother's arms.
  Deep down inside me, I am as content as a young child.

Israel, put your hope in the LORD
  both now and forever.

Psalm 133

*A song for those who go up to Jerusalem to worship
the LORD. A psalm of David.*

How good and pleasant it is
  when God's people live together in peace!
It's like the special olive oil
  that was poured on Aaron's head.
It ran down on his beard
  and on the collar of his robe.
It's as if the dew of Mount Hermon
  were falling on Mount Zion.
There the LORD gives his blessing.
  He gives life that never ends.

Psalm 136

Give thanks to the LORD, because he is good.
  His faithful love continues forever.
Give thanks to the greatest God of all.
  His faithful love continues forever.
Give thanks to the most powerful Lord of all.
  His faithful love continues forever.

Give thanks to the only one who can do great miracles.
  His faithful love continues forever.
By his understanding he made the heavens.
  His faithful love continues forever.
He spread out the earth on the waters.
  His faithful love continues forever.
He made the great lights in the sky.
  His faithful love continues forever.
He made the sun to rule over the day.
  His faithful love continues forever.
He made the moon and stars to rule over the night.
  His faithful love continues forever.

Give thanks to the God who killed the oldest son of each
    family in Egypt.
His faithful love continues forever.
He brought the people of Israel out of Egypt.
His faithful love continues forever.
He did it by reaching out his mighty hand and powerful arm.
His faithful love continues forever.

Give thanks to the God who parted the waters of the Red Sea.
His faithful love continues forever.
He brought Israel through the middle of it.
His faithful love continues forever.
But he swept Pharaoh and his army into the Red Sea.
His faithful love continues forever.

Give thanks to the God who led his people through the
    desert.
His faithful love continues forever.
He killed great kings.
His faithful love continues forever.
He struck down mighty kings.
His faithful love continues forever.
He killed Sihon, the king of the Amorites.
His faithful love continues forever.
He killed Og, the king of Bashan.
His faithful love continues forever.
He gave their land as a gift.
His faithful love continues forever.
He gave it as a gift to his servant Israel.
His faithful love continues forever.

Give thanks to the God who remembered us when things
    were going badly.
His faithful love continues forever.
He set us free from our enemies.
His faithful love continues forever.
He gives food to every creature.
His faithful love continues forever.

Give thanks to the God of heaven.
His faithful love continues forever.

Psalm 138

A psalm of David.

Lord, I will praise you with all my heart.
In front of those who think they are gods
I will sing praise to you.
I will bow down facing your holy temple.
I will praise your name,
because you are always loving and faithful.
You have honored your holy word
even more than your own fame.
When I called out to you, you answered me.
You made me strong and brave.

Lord, may all the kings on earth praise you
when they hear about what you have decided.
Lord, may they sing about what you have done,
because your glory is great.

Though the Lord is high above all, he cares for the lowly.
Though he is in heaven above, he sees them on earth
below.
Trouble is all around me,
but you keep me alive.
You reach out your hand to put a stop to the anger of my
enemies.
With your powerful right hand you save me.
Lord, you will show that I was right to trust you.
Lord, your faithful love continues forever.
You have done so much for us, so don't stop now.

remember what you read

1. What is something you noticed for the first time?

_____

_____

_____

_____

2. What questions did you have?

_____

_____

_____

_____

3. Was there anything that bothered you?

_____

_____

_____

_____

4. What did you learn about loving God?

_____

_____

_____

_____

5. What did you learn about loving others?

_____

_____

_____

_____

Psalm 139

For the director of music. A psalm of David.

L ORD, you have seen what is in my heart.
　You know all about me.
You know when I sit down and when I get up.
　You know what I'm thinking even though you are far
　　away.
You know when I go out to work and when I come back
　　home.
　You know exactly how I live.
L ORD, even before I speak a word,
　you know all about it.

You are all around me, behind me and in front of me.
　You hold me safe in your hand.
I'm amazed at how well you know me.
　It's more than I can understand.

How can I get away from your Spirit?
　Where can I go to escape from you?
If I go up to the heavens, you are there.
　If I lie down in the deepest parts of the earth, you are
　　also there.
Suppose I were to rise with the sun in the east.
　Suppose I travel to the west where it sinks into the
　　ocean.
Your hand would always be there to guide me.
　Your right hand would still be holding me close.

Suppose I were to say, "I'm sure the darkness will
    hide me.
  The light around me will become as dark as night."
Even that darkness would not be dark to you.
  The night would shine like the day,
  because darkness is like light to you.

You created the deepest parts of my being.
  You put me together inside my mother's body.
How you made me is amazing and wonderful.
  I praise you for that.
What you have done is wonderful.
  I know that very well.
None of my bones was hidden from you
  when you made me inside my mother's body.
  That place was as dark as the deepest parts of the
    earth.
When you were putting me together there,
  your eyes saw my body even before it was formed.
You planned how many days I would live.
  You wrote down the number of them in your book
  before I had lived through even one of them.

God, your thoughts about me are priceless.
  No one can possibly add them all up.
If I could count them,
  they would be more than the grains of sand.
If I were to fall asleep counting and then wake up,
  you would still be there with me.

God, I wish you would kill the people who are evil!
  I wish those murderers would get away from me!
They are your enemies. They misuse your name.
  They misuse it for their own evil purposes.
Lord, I really hate those who hate you!
  I really hate those who rise up against you!
I have nothing but hatred for them.
  I consider them to be my enemies.

God, see what is in my heart.
    Know what is there.
Test me.
    Know what I'm thinking.
See if there's anything in my life you don't like.
    Help me live in the way that is always right.

Psalm 141

A psalm of David.

I call out to you, LORD. Come quickly to help me.
    Listen to me when I call out to you.
May my prayer come to you like the sweet smell of incense.
    When I lift up my hands in prayer, may it be like the
        evening sacrifice.

LORD, guard my mouth.
    Keep watch over the door of my lips.
Don't let my heart be drawn to what is evil.
    Don't let me join with people who do evil.
    Don't let me eat their fancy food.

If a godly person hit me, it would be an act of kindness.
    If they would correct me, it would be like pouring olive oil
        on my head.
    I wouldn't say no to it.

I will always pray against the things that sinful people do.
    When their rulers are thrown down from the rocky cliffs,
    those evil people will realize that my words were true.
They will say, "As clumps of dirt are left from plowing up the
        ground,
    so our bones will be scattered near an open grave."

But LORD and King, I keep looking to you for help.
    I go to you for safety. Don't let me die.
Keep me from the traps of those who do evil.
    Save me from the traps they have set for me.
Let evil people fall into their own nets.
    But let me go safely on my way.

Psalm 143

A psalm of David.

LORD, hear my prayer.
Listen to my cry for mercy.
You are faithful and right.
Come and help me.
Don't take me to court and judge me,
because in your eyes no living person does what is
right.

My enemies chase me.
They crush me down to the ground.
They make me live in the darkness
like those who died long ago.
So I grow weak.
Deep down inside me, I'm afraid.

I remember what happened long ago.
I spend time thinking about all your acts.
I consider what your hands have done.
I spread out my hands to you in prayer.
I'm thirsty for you, just as dry ground is thirsty
for rain.

LORD, answer me quickly.
I'm growing weak.
Don't turn your face away from me,
or I will be like those who go down into the grave.
In the morning let me hear about your faithful love,
because I've put my trust in you.
Show me the way I should live,
because I trust you with my life.
LORD, save me from my enemies,
because I go to you for safety.
Teach me to do what you want,
because you are my God.
May your good Spirit
lead me on a level path.

Lord, bring yourself honor by keeping me alive.
　Because you do what is right, get me out of trouble.
Because your love is faithful, put an end to my enemies.
　Destroy all of them, because I serve you.

Psalm 146

Praise the Lord.

I will praise the Lord.
　I will praise the Lord all my life.
　I will sing praise to my God as long as I live.

Don't put your trust in human leaders.
　Don't trust in people who can't save you.
When they die, they return to the ground.
　On that day their plans come to nothing.

Blessed are those who depend on the God of Jacob for help.
　Blessed are those who put their hope in the Lord their
　　God.
He is the Maker of heaven and earth and the ocean.
　He made everything in them.
　He remains faithful forever.
He stands up for those who are treated badly.
　He gives food to hungry people.
The Lord sets prisoners free.
　The Lord gives sight to those who are blind.
The Lord lifts up those who feel helpless.
　The Lord loves those who do what is right.
The Lord watches over the outsiders who live in our land.
　He takes good care of children whose fathers have died.
　He also takes good care of widows.
But he causes evil people to fail
　in everything they do.

The Lord rules forever.
　The God of Zion will rule for all time to come.

Praise the Lord.

Psalm 148

Praise the LORD.

Praise the LORD from the heavens.
  Praise him in the heavens above.
Praise him, all his angels.
  Praise him, all his angels in heaven.
Praise him, sun and moon.
  Praise him, all you shining stars.
Praise him, you highest heavens.
  Praise him, you waters above the skies.
Let all of them praise the name of the LORD,
  because at his command they were created.
He established them for ever and ever.
  He gave them laws they will always have to obey.

Praise the LORD from the earth,
  you great sea creatures and all the deepest parts of the
    ocean.
Praise him, lightning and hail, snow and clouds.
  Praise him, you stormy winds that obey him.
Praise him, all you mountains and hills.
  Praise him, all you fruit trees and cedar trees.
Praise him, all you wild animals and cattle.
  Praise him, you small creatures and flying birds.
Praise him, you kings of the earth and all nations.
  Praise him, all you princes and rulers on earth.
Praise him, young men and women.
  Praise him, old men and children.

Let them praise the name of the LORD.
  His name alone is honored.
  His glory is higher than the earth and the heavens.
He has given his people a strong king.
  All his faithful people praise him for that gift.
  All the people of Israel are close to his heart.

Praise the LORD.

Psalm 150

Praise the LORD.

Praise God in his holy temple.
   Praise him in his mighty heavens.
Praise him for his powerful acts.
   Praise him because he is greater than anything else.
Praise him by blowing trumpets.
   Praise him with harps and lyres.
Praise him with tambourines and dancing.
   Praise him with stringed instruments and flutes.
Praise him with clashing cymbals.
   Praise him with clanging cymbals.

Let everything that has breath praise the LORD.

Praise the LORD.

remember what you read

1. What is something you noticed for the first time?

That in the Psalms David repeats alot the character traits about God.

2. What questions did you have?

What does it mean when it says don't put your trust in Human leaders?

3. Was there anything that bothered you?

No.

4. What did you learn about loving God?

That we should Praise God not just on sunday but all the time.

5. What did you learn about loving others?

That we should help others know that we shouldn't put our trust in human leaders but God.

LAMENTATIONS

introduction to Lamentations

The book of Lamentations has five of a special kind of very sad song. The people sang these songs after Babylon destroyed Jerusalem. Here are two of the songs. Notice there is some hope in the second song. This hope is placed exactly in the middle of the full book of Lamentations. This made the people feel better. They knew that even if everything was terrible around them, God still loved them. He would build Jerusalem again and bring back their nation.

The city of Jerusalem is so empty!
    She used to be full of people.
But now she's like a woman whose husband has died.
    She used to be great among the nations.
She was like a queen among the kingdoms.
    But now she is a slave.

Jerusalem weeps bitterly at night.
    Tears run down her cheeks.
    None of her friends comforts her.
All those who were going to help her
    have turned against her.
    They have become her enemies.

After Judah's people had suffered greatly,
    they were taken away as prisoners.
Now they live among the nations.
    They can't find any place to rest.

All those who were chasing them have caught up with them.
And they can't get away.

The roads to Zion are empty.
No one travels to her appointed feasts.
All the public places near her gates are deserted.
Her priests groan.
Her young women are sad.
And Zion herself weeps bitterly.

Her enemies have become her masters.
They have an easy life.
The Lord has brought suffering to Jerusalem
because her people have committed so many sins.
Her children have been taken away as prisoners.
Her enemies have forced her people to leave their homes.

The city of Zion used to be full of glory.
But now her glory has faded away.
Her princes are like deer.
They can't find anything to eat.
They are almost too weak to get away
from those who hunt them down.

Jerusalem's people are suffering and wandering.
They remember all the treasures
they used to have.
But they fell into the hands of their enemies.
And no one was there to help them.
Their enemies looked at them.
They laughed because Jerusalem had been destroyed.

Her people have committed many sins.
They have become impure.
All those who honored Jerusalem now look down on her.
They all look at her as if she were a naked woman.
The city groans and turns away in shame.

Her skirts are dirty.
She didn't think about how things might turn out.

Her fall from power amazed everyone.
  And no one was there to comfort her.
She said, "Lord, please pay attention to how much I'm
    suffering.
  My enemies have won the battle over me."

Jerusalem's enemies took away
  all her treasures.
Her people saw outsiders
  enter her temple.
The Lord had commanded them
  not to do that.

All Jerusalem's people groan
  as they search for bread.
They trade their treasures for food
  just to stay alive.
Jerusalem says, "Lord, look at me.
  Think about my condition.
  Everyone looks down on me."

Jerusalem also says, "All you who are passing by,
  don't you care about what has happened to me?
  Just look at my condition.
Has anyone suffered the way I have?
  The Lord has brought all this on me.
He has made me suffer.
  His anger has burned against me.

"He sent down fire from heaven.
  It went deep down into my bones.
He spread a net to catch me by the feet.
  He stopped me right where I was.
He made me empty.
  I am sick all the time.

"My sins have been made into a heavy yoke.
  They were woven together by his hands.
They have been placed on my neck.
  The Lord has taken away my strength.

He has handed me over to my enemies.
  I can't win the battle over them.

"The Lord has refused to accept
  any of my soldiers.
He has sent for an army
  to crush my young men.
I am like grapes in the Lord's winepress.
  He has stomped on me,
    even though I am his very own.

"That's why I am weeping.
  Tears are flowing from my eyes.
No one is near to comfort me.
  No one can heal my spirit.
My children don't have anything.
  My enemies are much too strong for me."

Zion reaches out her hands.
  But no one is there to comfort her people.
The Lord has ordered that
  the neighbors of Jacob's people would become their enemies.
    Jerusalem has become impure among them.

Jerusalem says, "The Lord always does what is right.
  But I refused to obey his commands.
Listen, all you nations.
  Pay attention to how much I'm suffering.
My young men and women
  have been taken away as prisoners.

"I called out to those who were going to help me.
  But they turned against me.
My priests and elders
  died in the city.
They were searching for food
  just to stay alive.

"Lord, see how upset I am!
  I am suffering deep down inside.

My heart is troubled.
  Again and again I have refused to obey you.
Outside the city, people are being killed by swords.
  Inside, there is nothing but death.

"People have heard me groan.
  But no one is here to comfort me.
My enemies have heard about all my troubles.
  What you have done makes them happy.
So please judge them, just as you said you would.
  Let them become like me.

"Please pay attention to all their sinful ways.
  Punish them as you have punished me.
  You judged me because I had committed so many sins.
I groan all the time.
  And my heart is weak."
I am a man who has suffered greatly.
  The LORD has used the Babylonians
  to punish my people.
He has driven me away. He has made me walk
  in darkness instead of light.
He has turned his powerful hand against me.
  He has done it again and again, all day long.

He has worn out my body.
  He has broken my bones.
He has surrounded me and attacked me.
  He has made me suffer bitterly.
  He has made things hard for me.
He has made me live in darkness
  like those who are dead and gone.

He has built walls around me, so I can't escape.
  He has put heavy chains on me.
I call out and cry for help.
  But he won't listen to me when I pray.
He has put up a stone wall to block my way.
  He has made my paths crooked.

He has been like a bear waiting to attack me.
  He has been like a lion hiding in the bushes.
He has dragged me off the path.
  He has torn me to pieces.
  And he has left me helpless.
He has gotten his bow ready to use.
  He has shot his arrows at me.

The arrows from his bag
  have gone through my heart.
My people laugh at me all the time.
  They sing and make fun of me all day long.
The Lord has made my life bitter.
  He has made me suffer bitterly.

He made me chew stones that broke my teeth.
  He has walked all over me in the dust.
I have lost all hope of ever having any peace.
  I've forgotten what good times are like.
So I say, "My glory has faded away.
  My hope in the Lord is gone."

I remember how I suffered and wandered.
  I remember how bitter my life was.
I remember it very well.
  My spirit is very sad deep down inside me.
But here is something else I remember.
  And it gives me hope.

The Lord loves us very much.
  So we haven't been completely destroyed.
  His loving concern never fails.
His great love is new every morning.
  Lord, how faithful you are!
I say to myself, "The Lord is everything I will ever need.
  So I will put my hope in him."

The Lord is good to those who put their hope in him.
  He is good to those who look to him.

It is good when people wait quietly
  for the LORD to save them.
It is good for a man to carry a heavy load of suffering
  while he is young.

Let him sit alone and not say anything.
  The LORD has placed that load on him.
Let him bury his face in the dust.
  There might still be hope for him.
Let him turn his cheek toward those who would slap him.
  Let him be filled with shame.

The Lord doesn't turn his back
  on people forever.
He might bring suffering.
  But he will also show loving concern.
  How great his faithful love is!
He doesn't want to bring pain
  or suffering to anyone.

Every time people crush prisoners under their feet,
  the Lord knows all about it.
When people refuse to give someone what they should,
  the Most High God knows it.
When people don't treat someone fairly,
  the Lord knows it.

Suppose people order something to happen.
  It won't happen unless the Lord has planned it.
Troubles and good things alike come to people
  because the Most High God has commanded them
    to come.
A person who is still alive shouldn't blame God
  when God punishes them for their sins.

Let's take a good look at the way we're living.
  Let's return to the LORD.
Let's lift up our hands to God in heaven.
  Let's pray to him with all our hearts.

Let's say, "We have sinned.
  We've refused to obey you.
  And you haven't forgiven us.

"You have covered yourself with the cloud of your anger.
  You have chased us.
  You have killed us without pity.
You have covered yourself with the cloud of your anger.
  Our prayers can't get through to you.
You have made us become like trash and garbage
  among the nations.

"All our enemies have opened their mouths wide
  to swallow us up.
We are terrified and trapped.
  We are broken and destroyed."
Streams of tears flow from my eyes.
  That's because my people are destroyed.

Tears will never stop flowing from my eyes.
  My eyes can't get any rest.
I'll weep until the Lord looks down from heaven.
  I'll cry until he notices my tears.
What I see brings pain to my spirit.
  All the women of my city are mourning.

Those who were my enemies for no reason at all
  hunted me down as if I were a bird.
They tried to end my life
  by throwing me into a deep pit.
  They threw stones down at me.
The water rose and covered my head.
  I thought I was going to die.

Lord, I called out to you.
  I called out from the bottom of the pit.
I prayed, "Please don't close your ears
  to my cry for help."
  And you heard my appeal.

You came near when I called out to you.
  You said, "Do not be afraid."

Lord, you stood up for me in court.
  You saved my life and set me free.
Lord, you have seen the wrong things
  people have done to me.
  Stand up for me again!
You have seen how my enemies
  have tried to get even with me.
  You know all about their plans against me.

Lord, you have heard them laugh at me.
  You know all about their plans against me.
You have heard my enemies
  whispering among themselves.
  They speak against me all day long.
Just look at them sitting and standing there!
  They sing and make fun of me.

Lord, pay them back.
  Punish them for what their hands have done.
Cover their minds with a veil.
  Put a curse on them!
Lord, get angry with them and hunt them down.
  Wipe them off the face of the earth.

remember what you read

1. What is something you noticed for the first time?

That throught this whole chapter the Isrealites haven't said sorry even though they addmited the had done wrong.

2. What questions did you have?

None

3. Was there anything that bothered you?

No

4. What did you learn about loving God?

That God doesn't punish us because he likes to, He does it so that we learn our lesson

5. What did you learn about loving others?

That if they are upset about being punished and they think that their parents do it for Fun we can say the don't want to punish you thy do it because they love you and want you to learn your lesson

SONG OF SONGS

introduction to Song of Songs

Song of Songs is a love song. The people of Israel sang it at weddings. The bride and groom were treated as queen and king for a day, so they sang these parts to each other. It is a celebration of the love married people have for each other.

⁓ᴓᴓ⌇

This is the greatest song Solomon ever wrote.

King Solomon says to the Shulammite woman
"You are my love.
    You are like a mare among Pharaoh's chariot horses.
Your earrings make your cheeks even more beautiful.
    Your strings of jewels make your neck even more lovely.
We will make gold earrings for you.
    We'll decorate them with silver."

"You are so beautiful, my love!
    So beautiful!
    Your eyes are like doves."

The woman says
"My love, among the young men
    you are like an apple tree among the trees of the forest.
I'm happy to sit in your shade.
    Your fruit tastes so sweet to me.
Lead me to the dinner hall.
    Let your banner of love be lifted high above me.

Give me some raisins to make me strong.
Give me some apples to make me feel like new again.
Our love has made me weak.
Your left arm is under my head.
Your right arm is around me.
Women of Jerusalem, make me a promise.
Let the antelopes and the does serve as witnesses.
Don't stir up love.
Don't wake it up until it's ready.

"Listen! I hear my love!
Look! Here he comes!
He's leaping across the mountains.
He's coming over the hills.
The one who loves me is like an antelope or a young deer.
Look! There he stands behind our wall.
He's gazing through the window.
He's peering through the screen.
He said to me, 'Rise up, my love.
Come with me, my beautiful one.
Look! The winter is past.
The rains are over and gone.
Flowers are appearing on the earth.
The season for singing has come.
The cooing of doves
is heard in our land.
The fig trees are producing their early fruit.
The flowers on the vines are giving off their sweet smell.
Rise up and come, my love.
Come with me, my beautiful one.'"

The king says
"You are like a dove in an opening in the rocks.
You are like a dove in a hiding place on a mountainside.
Show me your face.
Let me hear your voice.
Your voice is so sweet.
Your face is so lovely.

Catch the foxes for us.
  Catch the little foxes.
They destroy our vineyards.
  The vineyards are in bloom."

The woman says

  "My love belongs to me, and I belong to him.
    Like an antelope, he eats among the lilies.
  Until the day begins
    and the shadows fade away,
  turn to me, my love.
    Be like an antelope
  or like a young deer
    on the rocky hills.

Women of Jerusalem, make me a promise.
  Let the antelopes and the does serve as witnesses.
Don't stir up love.
  Don't wake it up until it's ready.

"Who is this man coming up from the desert
  like a column of smoke?
He smells like myrrh and incense
  made from all the spices of the trader.
Look! There's Solomon's movable throne.
  Sixty soldiers accompany it.
  They have been chosen from the best warriors in Israel.
All of them are wearing swords.
  They have fought many battles.
Each one has his sword at his side.
  Each is prepared for the terrors of the night.
King Solomon made the movable throne for himself.
  He made it out of wood from Lebanon.
He formed its posts out of silver.
  He made its base out of gold.
Its seat was covered with purple cloth.
  It was decorated inside with love.
  Women of Jerusalem, come out.

"Look, you women of Zion.
  Look at King Solomon wearing his crown.
  His mother placed it on him.
She did it on his wedding day.
  His heart was full of joy."

The king says to the Shulammite woman

"You are so beautiful, my love!
  So beautiful!
  Your eyes behind your veil are like doves.
Your hair flows like a flock of black goats
  coming down from the hills of Gilead.
Your teeth are as clean as a flock of sheep.
  Their wool has just been clipped.
  They have just come up from being washed.
Each of your teeth has its twin.
  Not one of them is alone.
Your lips are like a bright red ribbon.
  Your mouth is so lovely.
Your cheeks behind your veil
  are like the halves of a pomegranate.
Your neck is strong and beautiful like the tower of David.
  That tower is built with rows of stones.
A thousand shields are hanging on it.
  All of them belong to mighty soldiers.

"Come with me from Lebanon, my bride.
  Come with me from Lebanon.
Come down from the top of Mount Amana.
  Come down from the top of Senir.
  Come to me from the peak of Mount Hermon.
Leave the dens where the lions live.
  Leave the places in the mountains where the leopards
    stay.
My bride, you have stolen my heart
  with one glance of your eyes.
My sister, you have stolen my heart
  with one jewel in your necklace.

My bride, your love is so delightful.
  My sister, your love makes me happier than wine does.
  Your perfume smells better than any spice.
Your lips are as sweet as honey, my bride.
  Milk and honey are under your tongue.
  Your clothes smell like the cedar trees in Lebanon.
My bride, you are like a garden that is locked up.
  My sister, you are like a spring of water that has a fence
    around it.
  You are like a fountain that is sealed up.
You are like trees whose branches are loaded
  with pomegranates, fine fruits, henna and nard,
  with nard and saffron, cane and cinnamon.
You are like every kind of incense tree.
  You have myrrh, aloes
  and all the finest spices.
You are like a fountain in a garden.
  You are like a well of flowing water
  streaming down from Lebanon."

The woman says
  "Wake up, north wind!
    Come, south wind!
  Blow on my garden.
    Then its sweet smell will spread everywhere.
  Let my love come into his garden.
    Let him taste its fine fruits."

The king says
  "My bride, I have come into my garden.
    My sister, I've gathered my myrrh and my spice.
  I've eaten my honeycomb and my honey.
    I've drunk my wine and my milk."

The other women say to the Shulammite woman and to Solomon
  "Friends, eat and drink.
    Drink up all the love you want."

remember what you read

1. What is something you noticed for the first time?

That Soloman was very passionate about his Bride.

2. What questions did you have?

None

3. Was there anything that bothered you?

No.

4. What did you learn about loving God?

That God wants us to love who we marry forever.

5. What did you learn about loving others?

That we should love them.

introduction to Proverbs, parts 1-4

Proverbs are wise sayings. You might have heard, "An apple a day keeps the doctor away." This recent proverb doesn't mean if you eat an apple every day you won't ever need to see a doctor. It means, "If you choose healthy foods, you will probably be healthy." But it's more fun to say the rhyme about the apple.

In the same way, the proverbs in the Bible are not statements of fact. They are sayings that are easy to remember. They are usually true. Think about these wise sayings when you make choices. They will often help you make better choices. But they do not promise you exactly what will happen.

These are the proverbs of Solomon. He was the son of David and the king of Israel.

Proverbs teach you wisdom and instruct you.
> They help you understand wise sayings.
They provide you with instruction and help you live wisely.
> They lead to what is right and honest and fair.
They give understanding to childish people.
> They give knowledge and good sense to those who are young.
Let wise people listen and add to what they have learned.
> Let those who understand what is right get guidance.
What I'm teaching also helps you understand proverbs and stories.

It helps you understand the sayings and riddles of those
who are wise.

If you really want to gain knowledge, you must begin by
having respect for the LORD.
But foolish people hate wisdom and instruction.

⚬⚬⚬

Out in the open wisdom calls out.
She raises her voice in a public place.

"The wrong path that childish people take will kill
them.
Foolish people will be destroyed by being satisfied
with the way they live.
But those who listen to me will live in safety.
They will be at ease and have no fear of being harmed."

My son, accept my words.
Store up my commands inside you.
Let your ears listen to wisdom.
Apply your heart to understanding.
Call out for the ability to be wise.
Cry out for understanding.
Look for it as you would look for silver.
Search for it as you would search for hidden treasure.
Then you will understand how to have respect for the
LORD.
You will find out how to know God.
The LORD gives wisdom.
Knowledge and understanding come from his mouth.
He stores up success for honest people.
He is like a shield to those who live without blame.
He guards the path of those who are honest.
He watches over the way of his faithful ones.

You will understand what is right and honest and fair.
You will understand the right way to live.

Your heart will become wise.
　　Your mind will delight in knowledge.
Good sense will keep you safe.
　　Understanding will guard you.

Wisdom will save you from the ways of evil men.
　　It will save you from men who twist their words.
Men like that have left the straight paths
　　to walk in dark ways.
They take delight in doing what is wrong.
　　They take joy in twisting everything around.
Their paths are crooked.
　　Their ways are not straight.

My son, do not forget my teaching.
　　Keep my commands in your heart.
They will help you live for many years.
　　They will bring you peace and success.

Don't let love and truth ever leave you.
　　Tie them around your neck.
　　Write them on the tablet of your heart.
Then you will find favor and a good name
　　in the eyes of God and people.

Trust in the Lord with all your heart.
　　Do not depend on your own understanding.
In all your ways obey him.
　　Then he will make your paths smooth and straight.

Don't be wise in your own eyes.
　　Have respect for the Lord and avoid evil.
That will bring health to your body.
　　It will make your bones strong.

Honor the Lord with your wealth.
　　Give him the first share of all your crops.
Then your storerooms will be so full they can't hold
　　　　everything.
　　Your huge jars will spill over with fresh wine.

My son, do not hate the Lord's training.
  Do not object when he corrects you.
The Lord trains those he loves.
  He is like a father who trains the son he is pleased with.

Blessed is the one who finds wisdom.
  Blessed is the one who gains understanding.
Wisdom pays better than silver does.
  She earns more than gold does.
She is worth more than rubies.
  Nothing you want can compare with her.
Long life is in her right hand.
  In her left hand are riches and honor.
Her ways are pleasant ways.
  All her paths lead to peace.
She is a tree of life to those who take hold of her.
  Those who hold her close will be blessed.

By wisdom the Lord laid the earth's foundations.
  Through understanding he set the heavens in place.
By his knowledge the seas were separated,
  and the clouds dropped their dew.

My sons, listen to a father's teaching.
  Pay attention and gain understanding.
I give you good advice.
  So don't turn away from what I teach you.
I, too, was once a young boy in my father's house.
  And my mother loved me deeply.
Then my father taught me.
  He said to me, "Take hold of my words with all your heart.
  Keep my commands, and you will live.
Get wisdom, and get understanding.
  Don't forget my words or turn away from them.
Stay close to wisdom, and she will keep you safe.
  Love her, and she will watch over you.
To start being wise you must first get wisdom.
  No matter what it costs, get understanding.

Value wisdom highly, and she will lift you up.
　　Hold her close, and she will honor you.
She will set a beautiful crown on your head.
　　She will give you a glorious crown."

You people who don't want to work, think about the ant!
　　Consider its ways and be wise!
It has no commander.
　　It has no leader or ruler.
But it stores up its food in summer.
　　It gathers its food at harvest time.

You lazy people, how long will you lie there?
　　When will you get up from your sleep?
You might sleep a little or take a little nap.
　　You might even fold your hands and rest.
Then you would be poor, as if someone had robbed you.
　　You would have little, as if someone had stolen from you.

An evil troublemaker
　　goes around saying twisted things with his mouth.
He winks with his eyes.
　　He makes signals with his feet.
He motions with his fingers.
　　His plans are evil, and he has lies in his heart.
He is always stirring up fights.
Trouble will catch up with him in an instant.
　　He will suddenly be destroyed, and nothing can save him.

There are six things the Lord hates.
　　In fact, he hates seven things.
　　　　The Lord hates proud eyes,
　　　　a lying tongue,
　　　　and hands that kill those who aren't guilty.
　　　　He also hates hearts that make evil plans
　　　　and feet that are quick to do evil.
　　　　He hates any witness who pours out lies
　　　　and anyone who stirs up conflict in the community.

If you want to become wise, you must begin by respecting
      the LORD.
   To know the Holy One is to gain understanding.
Through wisdom, you will live a long time.
   Years will be added to your life.
If you are wise, your wisdom will reward you.
   If you make fun of others, you alone will suffer.

remember what you read

1. What is something you noticed for the first time?

That the first thing you need for
wisdom is to have respect for
the Lord

2. What questions did you have?

None

3. Was there anything that bothered you?

No

4. What did you learn about loving God?

That God doesn't want us to
lie commit murder. He wants us
to follow him.

5. What did you learn about loving others?

That if someone is lazy we could
share the paragraph about the ant.

These are the proverbs of Solomon.

A wise son makes his father glad.
  But a foolish son brings sorrow to his mother.

Riches that are gained by sinning aren't worth anything.
  But doing what is right saves you from death.

The Lord gives those who do right the food they need.
  But he lets those who do wrong go hungry.

Hands that don't want to work make you poor.
  But hands that work hard bring wealth to you.

A child who gathers crops in summer is wise.
  But a child who sleeps at harvest time brings shame.

A wise heart accepts commands.
  But foolish chattering destroys you.

Hate stirs up fights.
  But love erases all sins by forgiving them.

Wisdom is found on the lips of those who understand what is
    right.
  But those who have no sense are punished.

Wise people store up knowledge.
  But the mouths of foolish people destroy them.

The wealth of rich people is like a city that makes them feel
    safe.
  But having nothing destroys those who are poor.

People who do what is right earn life.
But sinners earn sin and death.

Anyone who pays attention to correction
shows the path to life.
But anyone who refuses to be corrected
leads others down the wrong path.

Anyone who hides hatred with lying lips
and spreads lies is foolish.

Sin is not ended by using many words.
But those who are wise control their tongues.

The mouths of those who do right produce wisdom.
But tongues that speak twisted words will be made
silent.

Those who do right know the proper thing to say.
But those who do wrong speak only twisted words.

The Lord hates it when people use scales to cheat others.
But he is delighted when people use honest weights.

When pride comes, shame follows.
But wisdom comes to those who are not proud.

Those who do what is right are guided by their honest lives.
But those who aren't faithful are destroyed by their lies.

Wealth isn't worth anything when God judges you.
But doing what is right saves you from death.

The ways of honest people are made straight because they
do what is right.
But those who do what is wrong are brought down by their
own sins.

Godly people are saved by doing what is right.
But those who aren't faithful are trapped by evil longings.

Hopes placed in human beings will die with them.
Everything their power promised comes to nothing.

Whoever makes fun of their neighbor has no sense.
But the one who has understanding controls their
tongue.

Those who talk about others will tell secrets.
But those who can be trusted keep the secrets of others.

Without guidance a nation falls.
But many good advisers can bring victory to a nation.

One person gives freely but gets even richer.
Another person doesn't give what they should but gets
even poorer.

Anyone who gives a lot will succeed.
Anyone who renews others will be renewed.

Anyone who loves correction loves knowledge.
Anyone who hates to be corrected is stupid.

The Lord blesses anyone who does good.
But he judges anyone who plans to do evil.

No one can become strong and steady by doing evil.
But if people do what is right, they can't be removed
from the land.

An excellent woman is her husband's crown.
But a wife who brings shame is like sickness in his bones.

The plans of godly people are right.
But the advice of sinners will lead you the wrong way.

The words of those who are evil hide and wait to spill
people's blood.
But the speech of those who are honest saves them from
traps like that.

Sinners are destroyed and taken away.
But the houses of godly people stand firm.

A person is praised for how wise they are.
But people hate anyone who has a twisted mind.

Those who do what is wrong are safe for just a while.
But those who do what is right last forever.

Those who do evil are trapped by their sinful talk.
But those who have done no wrong escape trouble.

Many good things come from what people say.
And the work of their hands rewards them.

The way of foolish people seems right to them.
But those who are wise listen to advice.

Foolish people are easily upset.
But wise people pay no attention to hurtful words.

An honest witness tells the truth.
But a dishonest witness tells lies.

The words of thoughtless people cut like swords.
But the tongue of wise people brings healing.

Truthful words last forever.
But lies last for only a moment.

There are lies in the hearts of those who plan evil.
But there is joy for those who work to bring peace.

Wise people keep their knowledge to themselves.
But the hearts of foolish people shout foolish things.

Hands that work hard will rule.
But people who are lazy will be forced to work.

Worry makes the heart heavy.
But a kind word cheers it up.

Godly people are careful about the friends they choose.
But the way of sinners leads them down the wrong
    path.

Those who guard what they say guard their lives.
But those who speak without thinking will be
    destroyed.

People who refuse to work want things and get nothing.
  But the desires of people who work hard are completely
    satisfied.

Where there is arguing, there is pride.
  But those who take advice are wise.

Money gained in the wrong way disappears.
  But money gathered little by little grows.

Hope that is put off makes one sick at heart.
  But a desire that is met is like a tree of life.

Anyone who hates what they are taught will pay for it later.
  But a person who respects a command will be rewarded.

The teaching of wise people is like a fountain that gives life.
  It turns those who listen to it away from the jaws of
    death.

Good judgment wins favor.
  But the way of liars leads to their ruin.

Walk with wise people and become wise.
  A companion of foolish people suffers harm.

A wise woman builds her house.
  But a foolish woman tears hers down with her own
    hands.

Whoever has respect for the Lord lives a good life.
  But those who hate him walk down an evil path.

The proud words of a foolish person sting like a whip.
  But the things wise people say keep them safe.

Those who make fun of others look for wisdom and don't
    find it.
  But knowledge comes easily to those who understand what
    is right.

Stay away from a foolish person.
  You won't find knowledge in what they say.

People are wise and understanding when they think about
the way they live.
But people are foolish when their foolish ways trick them.

Foolish people laugh at making things right when they sin.
But honest people try to do the right thing.

There is a way that appears to be right.
But in the end it leads to death.

Anyone who gets angry quickly does foolish things.
And a person who is tricky is hated.

Childish people act in keeping with their foolish ways.
But knowledge makes wise people feel like kings.

Those who plan evil go down the wrong path.
But those who plan good find love and truth.

All hard work pays off.
But if all you do is talk, you will be poor.

Anyone who is patient has great understanding.
But anyone who gets angry quickly shows how foolish
they are.

A peaceful heart gives life to the body.
But jealousy rots the bones.

Anyone who crushes poor people makes fun of their Maker.
But anyone who is kind to those in need honors God.

When trouble comes, sinners are brought down.
But godly people seek safety in God even as they die.

A gentle answer turns anger away.
But mean words stir up anger.

The tongues of wise people use knowledge well.
But the mouths of foolish people pour out foolish words.

The eyes of the Lord are everywhere.
They watch those who are evil and those who are good.

People who make fun of others don't like to be corrected.
 So they stay away from wise people.

A happy heart makes a face look cheerful.
 But a sad heart produces a broken spirit.

It is better to have respect for the LORD and have little
 than to be rich and have trouble.

A few vegetables where there is love
 are better than the finest meat where there is hatred.

A person with a bad temper stirs up conflict.
 But a person who is patient calms things down.

The hearts of those who do right think about how they will
   answer.
 But the mouths of those who do wrong pour out evil.

The LORD is far away from those who do wrong.
 But he hears the prayers of those who do right.

remember what you read

1. What is something you noticed for the first time?

That foolish people no matter what are
always going to fail unless they turn to
God.

2. What questions did you have?

Who wrote the book of Proverbs?

3. Was there anything that bothered you?

No.

4. What did you learn about loving God?

That God doesn't want us to foolish
people and be far away from him, He
wants us to be wise people and love
and follow him.

5. What did you learn about loving others?

That if you see two people fighting
you could go over and help stop
the agurement because it does
them no good.

WISDOM

The cheerful look of a messenger brings joy to your heart.
And good news gives health to your body.

Whoever listens to a warning that gives life
will be at home among those who are wise.

Those who turn away from correction hate themselves.
But anyone who accepts correction gains understanding.

Wisdom teaches you to have respect for the LORD.
So don't be proud if you want to be honored.

People make plans in their hearts.
But the LORD puts the correct answer on their tongues.

Everything a person does might seem pure to them.
But the LORD knows why they do what they do.

Commit to the LORD everything you do.
Then he will make your plans succeed.

The LORD works everything out to the proper end.
Even those who do wrong were made for a day of
trouble.

The LORD hates all those who have proud hearts.
You can be sure that they will be punished.

Through love and truth sin is paid for.
People avoid evil when they have respect for the LORD.

When the way you live pleases the LORD,
he makes even your enemies live at peace with you.

It is better to have a little and do right
    than to have a lot and be unfair.

In their hearts human beings plan their lives.
    But the Lord decides where their steps will take them.

Suppose you are lowly in spirit along with those who are
        treated badly.
    That's better than sharing stolen goods with those who
        are proud.

If anyone pays attention to what they're taught, they will
        succeed.
    Blessed is the person who trusts in the Lord.

Wise hearts are known for understanding what is right.
    Kind words make people want to learn more.

Kind words are like honey.
    They are sweet to the spirit and bring healing to the body.

There is a way that appears to be right.
    But in the end it leads to death.

A twisted person stirs up conflict.
    Anyone who talks about others separates close friends.

A person who wants to hurt others tries to get them to sin.
    That person leads them down a path that isn't good.

Whoever winks with their eye is planning to do wrong.
    Whoever closes their lips tightly is up to no good.

It is better to eat a dry crust of bread in peace and quiet
    than to eat a big dinner in a house full of fighting.

Evil people listen to lies.
    Lying people listen to evil.

Anyone who laughs at those who are poor makes fun
        of their Maker.
    Anyone who is happy when others suffer will be
        punished.

Whoever wants to show love forgives a wrong.
But those who talk about it separate close friends.

Starting to argue is like making a crack in a dam.
So drop the matter before a fight breaks out.

A friend loves at all times.
They are there to help when trouble comes.

The one who loves to argue loves to sin.
The one who builds a high gate is just asking to be
destroyed.

We think even foolish people are wise if they keep silent.
We think they understand what is right if they control their
tongues.

A person who isn't friendly looks out only for themselves.
They oppose all good sense by starting fights.

Foolish people don't want to understand.
They take delight in saying only what they think.

The name of the Lord is like a strong tower.
Godly people run to it and are safe.

If a person's heart is proud, they will be destroyed.
So don't be proud if you want to be honored.

To answer before listening
is foolish and shameful.

A cheerful spirit gives strength even during sickness.
But you can't keep going if you have a broken spirit.

Your tongue has the power of life and death.
Those who love to talk will eat the fruit of their words.

The one who finds a wife finds what is good.
He receives favor from the Lord.

It is better to be poor and to live without blame
than to be foolish and to twist words around.

Getting excited about something without knowledge isn't
good.
It's even worse to be in a hurry and miss the way.

A person's own foolish acts destroy their life.
But their heart is angry with the LORD.

Anyone who doesn't want to work sleeps his life away.
And a person who refuses to work goes hungry.

Those who keep commandments keep their lives.
But those who don't care how they live will die.

Anyone who is kind to poor people lends to the LORD.
God will reward them for what they have done.

Train your children, because then there is hope.
Don't do anything to bring about their deaths.

A person with a bad temper must pay for it.
If you save them, you will have to do it again.

Listen to advice and accept correction.
In the end you will be counted among those who
are wise.

A person who doesn't want to work leaves his hand in
the dish.
He won't even bring it back up to his mouth!

Don't love sleep, or you will become poor.
Stay awake, and you will have more food than you
need.

"It's no good. It's no good!" says a buyer.
Then off they go and brag about what they bought.

There is gold, and there are plenty of rubies.
But lips that speak knowledge are a priceless jewel.

Food gained by cheating tastes sweet.
But you will end up with a mouth full of gravel.

Plans are made by asking for guidance.
So if you go to war, get good advice.

A person who talks about others tells secrets.
So avoid anyone who talks too much.

The LORD directs a person's steps.
So how can anyone understand their own way?

A person is trapped if they make a hasty promise to God
and only later thinks about what they said.

Do what is right and fair.
The LORD accepts that more than sacrifices.

The proud eyes and hearts of sinful people are like a field not
plowed.
Those things produce nothing good.

The plans of people who work hard succeed.
You can be just as sure that those in a hurry will become
poor.

A fortune made by people who tell lies
amounts to nothing and leads to death.

Whoever refuses to listen to the cries of poor people
will also cry out and not be answered.

When you do what is fair, you make godly people glad.
But you terrify those who do what is evil.

Sinful people try to look as if they were bold.
But honest people think about how they live.

No wisdom, wise saying or plan
can succeed against the LORD.

You can prepare a horse for the day of battle.
But the power to win comes from the LORD.

You should want a good name more than you want great riches.
To be highly respected is better than having silver or gold.

Start children off on the right path.
  And even when they are old, they will not turn away
    from it.

Rich people rule over those who are poor.
  Borrowers are slaves to lenders.

Anyone who plants evil gathers a harvest of trouble.
  Their power to treat others badly will be destroyed.

Those who give freely will be blessed.
  That's because they share their food with those who are
    poor.

If you drive away those who make fun of others, fighting also
    goes away.
  Arguing and unkind words will stop.

People who don't want to work say, "There's a lion outside!"
  Or they say, "I'll be murdered if I go out into the streets!"

Children are going to do foolish things.
  But correcting them will drive that foolishness far away.

You might treat poor people badly or give gifts to rich people.
  Trying to get rich in these ways will instead make you poor.

remember what you read

1. What is something you noticed for the first time?

If you go your way you won't succeed.

2. What questions did you have?

None.

3. Was there anything that bothered you?

No.

4. What did you learn about loving God?

That we should listen to God and respect Him. Not ignore Him.

5. What did you learn about loving others?

That we shouldn't Give gifts to rich people just so that they will give us things back So we can get rich

Don't be a friend of a person who has a bad temper.
Don't go around with a person who gets angry easily.
You might learn their habits.
And then you will be trapped by them.

Do you see someone who does good work?
That person will serve kings.
That person won't serve officials of lower rank.

Don't wear yourself out to get rich.
Don't trust how wise you think you are.
When you take even a quick look at riches, they are gone.
They grow wings and fly away into the sky like an eagle.

Don't speak to foolish people.
They will laugh at your wise words.

Do not want what evil people have.
Don't long to be with them.
In their hearts they plan to hurt others.
With their lips they talk about making trouble.

Anyone who thinks up sinful things to do
will be known as one who plans evil.
Foolish plans are sinful.
People hate those who make fun of others.

Don't be happy when your enemy falls.
When he trips, don't let your heart be glad.
The Lord will see it, but he won't be pleased.
He might turn his anger away from your enemy.

Don't be upset because of evil people.
  Don't long for what sinners have. *Need to work on*
Tomorrow evil people won't have any hope.
  The lamps of sinners will be blown out.

⁓⁓⁓

Don't brag in front of the king.
  Don't claim a place among his great men.
Let the king say to you, "Come up here."
  That's better than for him to shame you in front of his
    nobles.

If you find honey, eat just enough.
  If you eat too much of it, you will throw up.
Don't go to your neighbor's home very often.
  If they see too much of you, they will hate you.

If your enemy is hungry, give him food to eat.
  If he is thirsty, give him water to drink.
By doing these things, you will pile up burning coals on his
    head.
  And the LORD will reward you.

Like a north wind that brings rain you didn't expect
  is a crafty tongue that brings looks of shock.

Hearing good news from a land far away
  is like drinking cold water when you are tired.

Foolish people who do the same foolish things again
  are like a dog that returns to where it has thrown up.

Do you see a person who is wise in their own eyes?
  There is more hope for a foolish person than for them.

Don't be quick to get mixed up in someone else's fight.
  That's like grabbing a stray dog by its ears.

Suppose a crazy person shoots
  flaming arrows that can kill.

Someone who lies to their neighbor
and says, "I was only joking!" is just like that crazy person.

If you don't have wood, your fire goes out.
If you don't talk about others, arguing dies down.

Coal glows, and wood burns.
And a person who argues stirs up conflict.

Don't brag about tomorrow.
You don't know what a day will bring.

Let another person praise you, and not your own mouth.
Let an outsider praise you, and not your own lips.

Stones are heavy, and sand weighs a lot.
But letting a foolish person make you angry is a heavier
load than both of them.

Wounds from a friend can be trusted.
But an enemy kisses you many times.

When you are full, you even hate honey.
When you are hungry, even what is bitter tastes sweet.

Suppose you loudly bless your neighbor early in the
morning.
Then you might as well be cursing him.

A nagging wife is like the dripping
of a leaky roof in a rainstorm.
Stopping her is like trying to stop the wind.
It's like trying to grab olive oil with your hand.

As iron sharpens iron,
so one person sharpens another.

When you look into water, you see a likeness of your face.
When you look into your heart, you see what you are really
like.

Death and the Grave are never satisfied.
People's eyes are never satisfied either.

A country has many rulers when its people don't obey.
But an understanding ruler knows how to keep order.

A ruler who treats poor people badly
is like a pounding rain that leaves no crops.

A child who understands what is right learns from
instruction.
But a child who likes to eat too much brings shame on his
father.

When godly people win, everyone is very happy.
But when sinners take charge, everyone hides.

Anyone who hides their sins doesn't succeed.
But anyone who admits their sins and gives them up
finds mercy.

An evil person who rules over helpless people
is like a roaring lion or an angry bear.

Those who work their land will have plenty of food.
But those who chase dreams will be very poor.

A faithful person will be richly blessed.
But anyone who wants to get rich will be punished.

Those who won't share what they have want to get rich.
They don't know they are going to be poor.

It is better to warn a person than to pretend to praise
them.
In the end that person will be more pleased with you.

Anyone who steals from their parents and says, "It's not
wrong,"
is just like someone who destroys.

People who always want more stir up conflict.
But those who trust in the Lord will succeed.

Those who trust in themselves are foolish.
But those who live wisely are kept safe.

Those who give to poor people will have all they need.
But those who close their eyes to the poor will receive
many curses.

When those who are evil take charge, other people hide.
But when those who are evil die, godly people grow
stronger.

Whoever still won't obey after being warned many times
will suddenly be destroyed. Nothing can save them.

When those who do right grow stronger, the people are glad.
But when those who do wrong become rulers, the people
groan.

Those who make fun of others stir up a city.
But wise people turn anger away.

Suppose a wise person goes to court with a foolish person.
Then the foolish person gets mad and pokes fun, and there
is no peace.

Murderers hate honest people.
They try to kill those who do what is right.

Foolish people let their anger run wild.
But wise people keep themselves under control.

If rulers listen to lies,
all their officials become evil.

Have you seen someone who speaks without thinking?
There is more hope for foolish people than for that
person.

Pride brings a person low.
But those whose spirits are low will be honored.

Those who do what is right hate dishonest people.
Those who do what is wrong hate honest people.

These sayings are the words of Agur, son of Jakeh. These sayings came from God.

"Lᴏʀᴅ, I ask you for two things.
  Don't refuse me before I die.
Keep lies far away from me.
  Don't make me either poor or rich,
    but give me only the bread I need each day.
If you don't, I might have too much.
  Then I might say I don't know you.
  I might say, 'Who is the Lᴏʀᴅ?'
Or I might become poor and steal.
  Then I would bring shame to the name of my God.

"Do you do foolish things?
  Do you think you are better than others?
Do you plan evil?
  If you do, put your hand over your mouth and stop
    talking!
If you churn cream, you will produce butter.
  If you twist a nose, you will produce blood.
  And if you stir up anger, you will produce a fight."

Who can find an excellent woman?
  She is worth far more than rubies.
Her husband trusts her completely.
  She gives him all the important things he needs.
She brings him good, not harm,
  all the days of her life.
She chooses wool and flax.
  She loves to work with her hands.
She is like the ships of traders.
  She brings her food from far away.
She gets up while it is still night.
  She provides food for her family.
  She also gives some to her female servants.

She considers a field and buys it.
  She uses some of the money she earns to plant a vineyard.
She gets ready to work hard.
  Her arms are strong.
She sees that her trading earns a lot of money.
  Her lamp doesn't go out at night.
With one hand she holds the wool.
  With the other she spins the thread.
She opens her arms to those who are poor.
  She reaches out her hands to those who are needy.
When it snows, she's not afraid for her family.
  All of them are dressed in the finest clothes.
She makes her own bed coverings.
  She is dressed in fine linen and purple clothes.
Her husband is respected at the city gate.
  There he takes his seat among the elders of the land.
She makes linen clothes and sells them.
  She supplies belts to the traders.
She puts on strength and honor as if they were her clothes.
  She can laugh at the days that are coming.
She speaks wisely.
  She teaches faithfully.
She watches over family matters.
  She is busy all the time.
Her children stand up and call her blessed.
  Her husband also rises up, and he praises her.
He says, "Many women do excellent things.
  But you are better than all the others."
Charm can fool you. Beauty fades.
  But a woman who has respect for the Lord should be
    praised.
Give her honor for all that her hands have done.
  Let everything she has done bring praise to her at the city
    gate.

remember what you read

1. What is something you noticed for the first time?

That what God wants us to do is really love others no matter what.

2. What questions did you have?

None

3. Was there anything that bothered you?

No

4. What did you learn about loving God?

That we should respect God by doing what He commands and one of those things is to love others and be kind to them no matter what.

5. What did you learn about loving others?

That if the one person is our enemy we should kill them with kindness.

ECCLESIASTES

Introduction to Ecclesiastes

You have just read many wise sayings in Proverbs. Remember that these are true most of the time. But sometimes bad things happen to good people. Sometimes people who hurt others seem to have a good life with no problems. The Teacher in Ecclesiastes was upset by this. So this book struggles with why things don't work out the way we want them to. It is deeper thinking about wisdom. He talks about things being "meaningless." Be sure to read all of Ecclesiastes to understand what he means by this.

~~~

These are the words of the Teacher. He was the son of David. He was also the king in Jerusalem.

"Meaningless! Everything is meaningless!"
　　says the Teacher.
"Everything is completely meaningless!
　　Nothing has any meaning."

~~~

I gave myself everything my eyes wanted.
　　There wasn't any pleasure that I refused to give myself.
I took delight in everything I did.
　　And that was what I got for all my work.
But then I looked over everything my hands had done.
　　I saw what I had worked so hard to get.

And nothing had any meaning.
It was like chasing the wind.
Nothing was gained on this earth.

There is a time for everything.
There's a time for everything that is done on earth.

There is a time to be born.
And there's a time to die.
There is a time to plant.
And there's a time to pull up what is planted.
There is a time to kill.
And there's a time to heal.
There is a time to tear down.
And there's a time to build up.
There is a time to weep.
And there's a time to laugh.
There is a time to be sad.
And there's a time to dance.
There is a time to scatter stones.
And there's a time to gather them.
There is a time to embrace someone.
And there's a time not to embrace.
There is a time to search.
And there's a time to stop searching.
There is a time to keep.
And there's a time to throw away.
There is a time to tear.
And there's a time to mend.
There is a time to be silent.
And there's a time to speak.
There is a time to love.
And there's a time to hate.
There is a time for war.
And there's a time for peace.

What do workers get for their hard work? I've seen the heavy load God has put on human beings. He has made everything beautiful in its time. He has also given people a sense of who he is. But they can't completely understand what God has done from beginning to end. People should be happy and do good while they live. I know there's nothing better for them to do than that. Each of them should eat and drink. People should be satisfied with all their hard work. That is God's gift to them. I know that everything God does will last forever. Nothing can be added to it. And nothing can be taken from it. God does that so people will have respect for him.

Everything that now exists has already been.
    And what is coming has existed before.
    God will judge those who treat others badly.

⚬⚬⚬

I looked and saw how much people were suffering on this earth.

I saw the tears of those who are suffering.
    They don't have anyone to comfort them.
Power is on the side of those who treat them badly.
    Those who are suffering don't have anyone to comfort
        them.
Then I announced that those
    who have already died
are happier than those
    who are still alive.
But someone who hasn't been born yet
    is better off than the dead or the living.
That's because that person hasn't seen the evil things
    that are done on earth.

Two people are better than one.
    They can help each other in everything they do.
Suppose either of them falls down.
    Then the one can help the other one up.

But suppose a person falls down and doesn't have anyone to
    help them up.
  Then feel sorry for that person!
Or suppose two people lie down together.
  Then they'll keep warm.
  But how can one person keep warm alone?
One person could be overpowered.
  But two people can stand up for themselves.
  And a rope made out of three cords isn't easily broken.

A poor but wise young man is better off than an old but foolish
king. That king doesn't pay attention to a warning anymore. The
young man might have come from prison to become king. Or he
might have been born poor within the kingdom but still became
king. I saw that everyone was following the young man who had
become the new king. At first, all the people served him when he
became king. But those who came later weren't pleased with the
way he was ruling. That doesn't have any meaning either. It's like
chasing the wind.

Anyone who loves money never has enough.
  Anyone who loves wealth is never satisfied with what
    they get.
  That doesn't have any meaning either.

As more and more goods are made,
  more and more people use them up.
So how can those goods benefit their owners?
  All they can do is look at them with desire.

The sleep of a worker is sweet.
  It doesn't matter whether they eat a little or a lot.
But the wealth of rich people
  keeps them awake at night.

I've seen something very evil on earth.

It's when wealth is stored up
  and then brings harm to its owners.

It's also when wealth is lost
   because of an unwise business deal.
Then there won't be anything left
   for the owners' children.
Everyone is born naked.
   They come into the world with nothing.
   And they go out of it with nothing.
They don't get anything from their work
   that they can take with them.

I have seen what is good. It is good for a person to eat and drink. It's good for them to be satisfied with their hard work on this earth. That's what they should do during the short life God has given them. That's what God made them for. Sometimes God gives a person wealth and possessions. God makes it possible for that person to enjoy them. God helps them accept the life he has given them. God helps them to be happy in their work. All these things are gifts from God. A person like that doesn't have to think about how their life is going. That's because God fills their heart with joy.

ᐧᔿᑉ

In my meaningless life here's what I've seen.

I've seen godly people dying
   even though they are godly.
And I've seen sinful people living a long time
   even though they are sinful.
Don't claim to be better than you are.
   And don't claim to be wiser than you are.
   Why destroy yourself?
Don't be too sinful.
   And don't be foolish.
   Why die before your time comes?
It's good to hold on to both of those things.
   Don't let go of either one.
Whoever has respect for God will avoid
   going too far in either direction.

Wisdom makes one wise person more powerful
    than ten rulers in a city.

It is true that there isn't anyone on earth
    who does only what is right and never sins.

Don't pay attention to everything people say.
    If you do, you might hear your servant cursing you.
Many times you yourself have cursed others.
    Deep down inside, you know that's true.

⁂

Go and enjoy your food. Be joyful as you drink your wine. God
has already approved what you do. Always wear white clothes
to show you are happy. Anoint your head with olive oil. You love
your wife. So enjoy life with her. Do it all the days of this meaningless life God has given you on earth. That's what he made you
for. That's what you get for all your hard work on earth. No matter
what you do, work at it with all your might. Remember, you are
going to the place of the dead. And there isn't any work or planning or knowledge or wisdom there.

⁂

Here's something else I've seen on this earth.

Races aren't always won by those who run fast.
    Battles aren't always won by those who are strong.
Wise people don't always have plenty of food.
    Clever people aren't always wealthy.
    Those who have learned a lot aren't always successful.
God controls the timing of every event.
    He also controls how things turn out.
People should listen to the quiet words
    of those who are wise.
That's better than paying attention to the shouts
    of a ruler of foolish people.

Wisdom is better than weapons of war.
  But one sinner destroys a lot of good.

When a person won't work, the roof falls down.
  Because of hands that aren't busy, the house leaks.

You don't know the path the wind takes.
  You don't know how a baby is made inside its mother.
So you can't understand how God works either.
  He made everything.

⁕

Remember your Creator.
  Remember him while you are still young.
Think about him before your times of trouble come.
  The years will come when you will say,
  "I don't find any pleasure in them."
That's when the sunlight will become dark.
  The moon and the stars will also grow dark.
  And the clouds will return after it rains.
Remember your Creator before those who guard the
      house tremble with old age.
  That's when strong men will be bent over.
The women who grind grain will stop because there are so
      few of them left.
  Those who look through the windows won't be able
      to see very well.
Remember your Creator before the front doors are
      closed.
  That's when the sound of grinding will fade away.
Old people will rise up when they hear birds singing.
  But they will barely hear any of their songs.
Remember your Creator before you become afraid of
      places that are too high.
  You will also be terrified because of danger in the
      streets.

Remember your Creator before the almond trees have buds
on them.
That's when grasshoppers will drag themselves along.
Old people will lose their desire.
That's when people will go to their dark homes in the grave.
And those who mourn for the dead will walk around in the
streets.

The Teacher was wise. He gave knowledge to people. He tried
out many proverbs. He thought about them carefully. Then he
wrote them down in order. He did his best to find just the right
words. And what he wrote was honest and true.

The sayings of those who are wise move people to take action.
Their collected sayings are like nails pounded in firm and deep.
These sayings are given to us by one shepherd. My son, be careful
not to pay attention to anything added to them.

Books will never stop being written. Too much studying makes
people tired.

Everything has now been heard.
And here's the final thing I want to say.
Have respect for God and obey his commandments.
This is what he expects of all human beings.
God will judge everything people do.
That includes everything they try to hide.
He'll judge everything, whether it's good or evil.

remember what you read

1. What is something you noticed for the first time?

That Solomen said don't wait till your old to remember God. do it now,

2. What questions did you have?

None

3. Was there anything that bothered you?

No

4. What did you learn about loving God?

That God is the only God and he is in control of everything.

5. What did you learn about loving others?

That if they are new and try to fit in by making them sound and look like they are better then they really are you could tell them that they don't have to change for us to like them. we like them for who they are

JOB, PART 1

introduction to Job, parts 1-5

The book of Job tells the story of a good man named Job who lived a long time ago. He suffered terribly. For most of the book Job is arguing with his friends about why he is suffering. Job wants to talk to God directly to find out why he is suffering if he is actually living in a right way. Remember that Ecclesiastes had deeper thinking about wisdom than Proverbs. The book of Job contains even deeper thinking about life. It helps us know that God works in ways we don't understand. He does this for reasons only he knows. Notice the poem in part 4 that talks about where wisdom is found.

There was a man who lived in the land of Uz. His name was Job. He was honest. He did what was right. He had respect for God and avoided evil. Job had seven sons and three daughters. He owned 7,000 sheep and 3,000 camels. He owned 500 pairs of oxen and 500 donkeys. He also had a large number of servants. He was the most important man among all the people in the east.

His sons used to give feasts in their homes on their birthdays. They would invite their three sisters to eat and drink with them. The time for enjoying good food would end. Then Job would make plans for his children to be made pure and "clean." He would sacrifice a burnt offering for each of them. He would do it early in the morning. He would think, "Perhaps my children have sinned. Maybe they have spoken evil things against God in their hearts." That's what Job always did for his children when he felt they had sinned.

One day angels came to the LORD. Satan also came with them. The LORD said to Satan, "Where have you come from?"

Satan answered, "From traveling all around the earth. I've been going from one end of it to the other."

Then the LORD said to Satan, "Have you thought about my servant Job? There isn't anyone on earth like him. He is honest. He does what is right. He has respect for God and avoids evil."

"You always give Job everything he needs," Satan replied. "That's why he has respect for you. Haven't you guarded him and his family? Haven't you taken care of everything he has? You have blessed everything he does. His flocks and herds are spread all through the land. But now reach out your hand and strike down everything he has. Then I'm sure he will speak evil things against you. In fact, he'll do it right in front of you."

The LORD said to Satan, "All right. I am handing everything he has over to you. But do not touch the man himself."

Then Satan left the LORD and went on his way.

One day Job's sons and daughters were at their oldest brother's house. They were enjoying good food and drinking wine. During that time a messenger came to Job. He said, "The oxen were plowing. The donkeys were eating grass near them. Then the Sabeans attacked us and carried off the animals. They killed some of the servants with their swords. I'm the only one who has escaped to tell you!"

While he was still speaking, a second messenger came. He said, "God sent lightning from the sky. It struck the sheep and killed them. It burned up some of the servants. I'm the only one who has escaped to tell you!"

While he was still speaking, a third messenger came. He said, "The Chaldeans separated themselves into three groups. They attacked your camels and carried them off. They killed the rest of the servants with their swords. I'm the only one who has escaped to tell you!"

While he was still speaking, a fourth messenger came. He said, "Your sons and daughters were at their oldest brother's house. They were enjoying good food and drinking wine. Suddenly a strong wind blew in from the desert. It struck the four corners of the house. The house fell down on your children. Now all of them are dead. I'm the only one who has escaped to tell you!"

After Job heard all these reports, he got up and tore his robe. He shaved his head. Then he fell to the ground and worshiped the LORD. He said,

"I was born naked.
And I'll leave here naked.
The LORD has given, and the LORD has taken away.
May the name of the LORD be praised."

In spite of everything, Job didn't sin by blaming God for doing anything wrong.

On another day angels came to the LORD. Satan also came to him along with them. The LORD said to Satan, "Where have you come from?"

Satan answered, "From traveling all around the earth. I've been going from one end of it to the other."

Then the LORD said to Satan, "Have you thought about my servant Job? There isn't anyone on earth like him. He is honest. He does what is right. He has respect for God and avoids evil. You tried to turn me against him. You wanted me to destroy him without any reason. But he still continues to be faithful."

Satan replied, "A man will give everything he has to save himself. So Job is willing to give up the lives of his family to save his own life. But now reach out your hand and strike his flesh and bones. Then I'm sure he will speak evil things against you. In fact, he'll do it right in front of you."

The LORD said to Satan, "All right. I am handing him over to you. But you must spare his life."

Then Satan left the LORD and went on his way. He sent painful sores on Job. They covered him from the bottom of his feet to the top of his head. He got part of a broken pot. He used it to scrape his skin. He did it while he was sitting in ashes.

His wife said to him, "Are you still continuing to be faithful to the LORD? Speak evil things against him and die!"

Job replied, "You are talking like a foolish woman. We accept good things from God. So we should also accept trouble when he sends it."

In spite of everything, Job didn't say anything that was sinful.

Job had three friends named Eliphaz the Temanite, Bildad the Shuhite, and Zophar the Naamathite. They heard about all the troubles that had come to Job. So they started out from their homes. They had agreed to meet together. They wanted to go and show their concern for Job. They wanted to comfort him. When they got closer to where he lived, they could see him. But they could hardly recognize him. They began to weep out loud. They tore their robes and sprinkled dust on their heads. Then they sat down on the ground with him for seven days and seven nights. No one said a word to him. That's because they saw how much he was suffering.

After a while, Job opened his mouth to speak. He cursed the day he had been born. He said,

"May the day I was born be wiped out.
    May the night be wiped away when people said, 'A boy is
        born!'

"Why didn't I die when I was born?
    Why didn't I die as I came out of my mother's body?

"Why should those who suffer ever be born?
    Why should life be given to those whose spirits are
        bitter?
Why is life given to a man like me?
    God hasn't told me what will happen to me.
    He has surrounded me with nothing but trouble.
Sighs have become my food every day.
    Groans pour out of me like water.
I don't have any peace and quiet.
    I can't find any rest. All I have is trouble."

Then Eliphaz the Temanite replied,

"Job, suppose someone tries to talk to you.
  Will that make you uneasy?
  I can't keep from speaking up.
Look, you taught many people.
  You made weak hands strong.
Your words helped those who had fallen down.
  You made shaky knees strong.
Now trouble comes to you. And you are unhappy about it.
  It strikes you down. And you are afraid.
Shouldn't you worship God and trust in him?
  Shouldn't your honest life give you hope?

"Here's something to think about.
  Have people who aren't guilty ever been wiped out?
  Have honest people ever been completely destroyed?
Here's what I've observed.
  People gather a crop from what they plant.
  If they plant evil and trouble, that's what they will
      harvest.

Hard times don't just grow out of the soil.
  Trouble doesn't jump out of the ground.
People are born to have trouble.
  And that's just as sure as sparks fly up.

"If I were you, I'd make my appeal to God.
  I'd bring my case to be judged by him.
He does wonderful things that can't be understood.
  He does miracles that can't even be counted.
He lifts up people who are lowly in spirit.
  He lifts up those who are sad.
  He keeps them safe.
He stops the evil plans of those who are clever.
  The work of their hands doesn't succeed.
Some people think they are so wise.
  But God catches them in their own tricks.
  He sweeps away the evil plans of sinful people.

"Blessed is the person God corrects.
So don't hate the Mighty One's training.
He wounds. But he also bandages up those he wounds.
He harms. But his hands also heal those he harms.

"We have carefully studied all these things.
And they are true.
So pay attention to them.
Apply them to yourself."

Job replied,

"I wish my great pain could be weighed!
I wish all my suffering could be weighed on scales!
I'm sure it would weigh more than the grains of sand on the
seashore.
No wonder I've been so quick to speak!
The Mighty One has shot me with his arrows.
I have to drink their poison.
God's terrors are aimed at me.

"I'm so weak that I no longer have any hope.
Things have gotten so bad that I can't wait for help
anymore.

"A person shouldn't stop being kind to a friend.
Anyone who does that stops showing respect for the
Mighty One.
But my friends have stopped being kind to me.
You see the horrible condition I'm in.
And that makes you afraid.

"God, remember that my life is only a breath.
I'll never be happy again.

"What are human beings that you think so much of them?
What are they that you pay so much attention to them?
You check up on them every morning.
You test them every moment.

If I've really sinned, tell me what I've done to you.
   You see everything we do.
Why do you shoot your arrows at me?
   Have I become a problem to you?
Why don't you forgive the wrong things I've done?
   Why don't you forgive me for my sins?
I'll soon lie down in the dust of my grave.
   You will search for me. But I'll be gone."

remember what you read

1. What is something you noticed for the first time?

That Job had way bigger problems then we
have and we normally cry out to God, but
Job instead he worshipped God instead.

2. What questions did you have?

None.

3. Was there anything that bothered you?

No.

4. What did you learn about loving God?

That God is going to give us problems in life,
but that doesn't mean we stop loving and
respecting him.

5. What did you learn about loving others?

If someone is feeling down you could tell them to
never stop worshiping the Lord. Because hard times
are going to come and it is all in God's hands.

Then Bildad the Shuhite replied,

"Job, how long will you talk like that?
  Your words don't have any meaning.
Does God ever treat people unfairly?
  Does the Mighty One make what is wrong
    appear to be right?
Your children sinned against him.
  So he punished them for their sin.
But seek God with all your heart.
  Make your appeal to the Mighty One.
Be pure and honest.
  And he will rise up and help you now.
  He'll give you everything you had before.
In the past, things went well with you.
  But in days to come, things will get even better.

"I'm sure God doesn't turn his back on anyone who is honest.
  And he doesn't help those who do what is evil.
He will fill your mouth with laughter.
  Shouts of joy will come from your lips.
Your enemies will put on shame as if it were clothes.
  The tents of sinful people will be gone."

Job replied,

"I'm sure that what you have said is true.
  But how can human beings prove to God they are not
    guilty?

They might wish to argue with him.
But they couldn't answer him
even once in a thousand times.
His wisdom is deep. His power is great.
No one opposes him and comes away unharmed.
He moves mountains, and they don't even know it.
When he is angry, he turns them upside down.
He shakes the earth loose from its place.
He makes its pillars tremble.
When he tells the sun not to shine, it doesn't.
He turns off the light of the stars.
He's the only one who can spread out the heavens.
He alone can walk on the waves of the ocean.
He made the Big Dipper and Orion.
He created the Pleiades and the southern stars.
He does wonderful things that can't be understood.
He does miracles that can't even be counted.

"So how can I disagree with God?
How can I possibly argue with him?
Even if I hadn't done anything wrong,
I couldn't answer him.
I could only beg my Judge to have mercy on me.

"Even though I'm honest,
I'm not concerned about myself.
I hate my own life.
It all amounts to the same thing. That's why I say,
'God destroys honest people and sinful people alike.'

"God isn't a mere human being like me. I can't answer him.
We can't take each other to court.
I wish someone would settle matters between us.
I wish someone would bring us together.
I wish someone would keep God from punishing me.
Then his terror wouldn't frighten me anymore.
I would speak up without being afraid of him.
But as things stand now, I can't do that.

"I'm sick of living.
　　So I'll talk openly about my problems.
　　I'll speak out because my spirit is bitter.
I say to God, 'Don't find me guilty.
　　Instead, tell me what charges
　　you are bringing against me.

" 'Your hands shaped me and made me.
　　So are you going to destroy me now?
You gave me life. You were kind to me.
　　You took good care of me. You watched over me.

" 'But here's what you hid in your heart.
　　Here's what you had on your mind.
If I sinned, you would be watching me.
　　You wouldn't let me go without punishing me.' "

Then Zophar the Naamathite replied,

"Don't all your words require an answer?
　　I'm sure that what you are saying can't be right.
Your useless talk won't keep us quiet.
　　Someone has to correct you when you make fun of
　　　　truth.
You say to God, 'My beliefs are perfect.
　　I'm pure in your sight.'
I wish God would speak.
　　I wish he'd answer you.
I wish he'd show you the secrets of wisdom.
　　After all, true wisdom has two sides.
Here's what I want you to know.
　　God has forgotten some of your sins.

"So commit yourself to God completely.
　　Reach out your hands to him for help.
Get rid of all the sin you have.
　　Don't let anything that is evil stay in your tent.
Then, free of those things, you can face others.
　　You can stand firm without being afraid."

Job replied,

"You people think you are the only ones who matter!
  You are sure that wisdom will die with you!
But I have a brain, just like you.
  I'm as clever as you are.
  In fact, everyone knows as much as you do.

"My friends laugh at me all the time,
  even though I called out to God and he answered.
My friends laugh at me,
  even though I'm honest and right.
People who have an easy life look down on those who have
    problems.
  They think trouble comes only to those whose feet are
    slipping.

"But ask the animals what God does.
  They will teach you.
Or ask the birds in the sky.
  They will tell you.
Or speak to the earth. It will teach you.
  Or let the fish in the ocean educate you.
Are there any of these creatures that don't know
  what the powerful hand of the Lord has done?
He holds the life of every creature in his hand.
  He controls the breath of every human being.
Our tongues tell us what tastes good and what doesn't.
  And our ears tell us what's true and what isn't.
Old people are wise.
  Those who live a long time have understanding.

"Wisdom and power belong to God.
  Advice and understanding also belong to him.
Strength and understanding belong to him.
  Those who tell lies and those who believe them also belong
    to him.
He removes the wisdom of rulers and leads them away.
  He makes judges look foolish.

He makes nations great, and then he destroys them.
   He makes nations grow, and then he scatters them.

"My eyes have seen everything God has done.
   My ears have heard it and understood it.
What you know, I also know.
   I'm as clever as you are.
In fact, I long to speak to the Mighty One.
   I want to argue my case with God.
But you spread lies about me and take away my good
      name.
   If you are trying to heal me,
   you aren't very good doctors!
I wish you would keep your mouths shut!
   Then people would think you were wise.
Listen to my case.
   Listen as I make my appeal.
Will you say evil things in order to help God?
   Will you tell lies for him?
Do you want to be on God's side?
   Will you argue his case for him?
Would it turn out well if he looked you over carefully?
   Could you fool him as you might fool human beings?
He would certainly hold you responsible
   if you took his side in secret.
Wouldn't his glory terrify you?
   Wouldn't the fear of him fall on you?
Your sayings are as useless as ashes.
   The answers you give are as weak as clay.

"So be quiet and let me speak.
   Then I won't care what happens to me.
Why do I put myself in danger?
   Why do I take my life in my hands?
Even if God kills me, I'll still put my hope in him.
   I'll argue my case in front of him.
No matter how things turn out,
   I'm sure I'll still be saved.

After all, no ungodly person
would dare to come into his court.

"God, I won't hide from you.
Here are the only two things I want.
Stop treating me this way.
And stop making me so afraid.
Then send for me, and I'll answer.
Or let me speak, and you reply.
How many things have I done wrong?
How many sins have I committed?
Show me my crime. Show me my sin.

"I wish you would hide me in a grave!
I wish you would cover me up until your anger passes by!
I wish you would set the time for me to spend in the
grave
and then bring me back up!

"Water wears away stones.
Storms wash away soil.
In the same way, you destroy a person's hope.
You overpower them completely, and then they're gone.
You change the way they look and send them to their
graves.
If their children are honored, they don't even know it.
If their children are dishonored, they don't even see it.
All they feel is the pain of their own bodies.
They are full of sadness only for themselves."

Then Eliphaz the Temanite replied,

"Job, would a wise person answer with a lot of meaningless
talk?
Would they fill their stomach with the hot east wind?
Would they argue with useless words?
Would they give worthless speeches?
But you even cause others to lose their respect for God.
You make it hard for them to be faithful to him.

Your sin makes you say evil things.
  You talk like people who twist the truth.
Your own mouth judges you, not mine.
  Your own lips witness against you.

"Aren't God's words of comfort enough for you?
  He speaks them to you gently.
Why have you let your wild ideas carry you away?
  Why do your eyes flash with anger?
Why do you get so angry with God?
  Why do words like those pour out of your mouth?

"Can human beings really be pure?
  Can those who are born really be right with God?

"Listen to me. I'll explain things to you.
  Let me tell you what I've seen.
Sinful people always suffer pain.
  Mean people suffer all their lives.
Instead of having children,
  ungodly people create suffering.
All they produce is evil.
  They are full of lies."

remember what you read

1. What is something you noticed for the first time?

That Job is angery and scared just like we would be, but yet he still loves God and is worshiping him.

2. What questions did you have?

None

3. Was there anything that bothered you?

No

4. What did you learn about loving God?

That God is going to bring trouble on us not because we sinned, but God is testing us and we should accept it and love God.

5. What did you learn about loving others?

That we could give encouraging words to others when they are going through a hard time

JOB, PART 3

Job replied,

"I've heard many of these things before.
  All of you are terrible at comforting me!
Your speeches go on forever.
  Won't they ever end?
What's wrong with you?
  Why do you keep on arguing?
If you and I changed places,
  I could say the same things you are saying.
I could make fine speeches against you.
  I could shake my head at you.
But what I might say would give you hope.
  My words of comfort would help you.

"If I speak, it doesn't help me.
  And if I keep quiet, my pain doesn't go away.
God has worn me out completely.
  He has destroyed my whole family.
God is angry with me.
  He attacks me and tears me up.
Everything was going well with me.
  But he broke me into pieces like a clay pot.

"I've sewed rough clothing over my skin.
  All I can do is sit here in the dust.
My face is red from crying.
  I have dark circles under my eyes.
But I haven't harmed anyone.
  My prayers to God are pure.

"Come on, all of you! Try again!
    I can't find a wise person among you.
My life is almost over. My plans are destroyed.
    Yet the desires of my heart
turn night into day.
    Even though it's dark,
    'Light is nearby.'
Will hope go down to the gates of death with me?
    Will we go down together into the dust of the grave?"

Then Bildad the Shuhite replied,

"Job, when will you stop these speeches of yours?
    Be reasonable! Then we can talk.
Why do you look at us as if we were cattle?
    Why do you think of us as being stupid?
Your anger is tearing you to pieces.
    Does the earth have to be deserted just to prove you are
        right?
    Must all the rocks be moved from their places?

"The lamps of sinful people are blown out.
    Their flames will never burn again.
They are driven from light into the place of darkness.
    They are thrown out of the world.
Their family dies out among their people.
    No one is left where they used to live.
What has happened to them shocks the people in the west.
    It terrifies the people in the east.
Now you know what the homes of sinners are like.
    Those who don't know God live in places like that."

Job replied,

"How long will you people make me suffer?
    How long will you crush me with your words?
You have already accused me many times.
    You have attacked me without feeling any shame.

Suppose it's true that I've gone down the wrong path.
    Then it's my concern, not yours.
Suppose you want to place yourselves above me.
    Suppose you want to use my shame to prove I'm wrong.
Then I want you to know that God hasn't treated me right.
    In fact, he has captured me in his net.

"Have pity on me, my friends! Please have pity!
    God has struck me down with his powerful hand.
Why do you chase after me as he does?
    Aren't you satisfied with what you have done to me
        already?

"You might say, 'Let's keep bothering Job.
    After all, he's the cause of all his suffering.'
But you should be afraid when God comes to judge you.
    He'll be angry. He'll punish you with his sword.
    Then you will know that he is the Judge."

Then Zophar the Naamathite replied,

"My troubled thoughts force me to answer you.
    That's because I'm very upset.
What you have just said dishonors me.
    So I really have to reply to you.

"I'm sure you must know how things have always been.
    They've been that way
        ever since human beings were placed on this earth.
Those who are evil are happy for only a short time.
    The joy of ungodly people lasts only for a moment.

"No matter how much they have,
    they always long for more.
    But their treasure can't save them.
There isn't anything left for them to eat up.
    Their success won't last.
While they are enjoying the good life,
    trouble will catch up with them.
    Terrible suffering will come on them.

When they've filled their stomachs,
   God will pour out his great anger on them.
   He'll strike them down with blow after blow.
Heaven will show their guilt to everyone.
   The earth will be a witness against them.
A flood will carry their houses away.
   Rushing water will wash them away
   on the day when God judges.
Now you know what God will do to sinful people.
   Now you know what he has planned for them."

Job replied,

"Listen carefully to what I'm saying.
   Let that be the comfort you people give me.
Put up with me while I speak.
   After I've spoken, you can make fun of me!

"I'm not arguing with mere human beings.
   So why shouldn't I be angry and uneasy?
Look at me and be shocked.
   Put your hand over your mouth and stop talking!
When I think about these things, I'm terrified.
   My whole body trembles.
Why do sinful people keep on living?
   The older they grow, the richer they get.
They see their children grow up around them.
   They watch their family grow larger.
Their homes are safe.
   They don't have to be afraid.
   God isn't punishing them.
But they say to God, 'Leave us alone!
   We don't want to know how you want us to live.
Who is the Mighty One? Why should we serve
      him?
   What would we get if we prayed to him?'
But they aren't in control of their own success.
   So I don't pay any attention to their plans.

People say, 'God stores up the punishment of evil people for
      their children.'
   But let God punish the evil people themselves.
   Then they'll learn a lesson from it.

"Some people die while they are still very strong.
   They are completely secure. They have an easy life.
Others die while their spirits are bitter.
   They've never enjoyed anything good.

"I know exactly what you people are thinking.
   I know you are planning to do bad things to me.
You are saying to yourselves,
   'Where is the great man's house now?
   Where are the tents where his evil family lived?'
Haven't you ever asked questions of those who travel?
   Haven't you paid any attention to their stories?
They'll tell you that sinful people
   are spared from the day of trouble.

"So how can you comfort me with your speeches?
   They don't make any sense at all.
   Your answers are nothing but lies!"

Then Eliphaz the Temanite replied,

"Can any person be of benefit to God?
   Can even a wise person be of any help to him?
Job, what pleasure would it give the Mighty One if you were
      right?
   What would he get if you were completely honest?

"You say you have respect for him.
   Is that why he corrects you?
   Is that why he brings charges against you?
Haven't you done many evil things?
   Don't you sin again and again?

"Job, obey God and be at peace with him.
   Then he will help you succeed.

Do what he teaches you to do.
   Keep his words in your heart.
If you return to the Mighty One,
   you will have what you had before.
But first you must remove
   everything that is evil far from your tent.
When people are brought low you will say, 'Lift them up!'
   Then God will help them.
He'll even save those who are guilty.
   He'll save them because your hands are clean."

Job replied,

"Even today my problems are more than I can handle.
   In spite of my groans, God's hand is heavy on me.
I wish I knew where I could find him!
   I wish I could go to the place where he lives!
I would state my case to him.
   I'd give him all my arguments.
Would he strongly oppose me?
   No. He wouldn't bring charges against me.
There honest people can prove to him they're not guilty.
   There my Judge would tell me once and for all that I'm
      not guilty.

"My feet have closely followed his steps.
   I've stayed on his path without turning away.
I haven't disobeyed his commands.
   I've treasured his words more than my daily bread.

"But he's the only God. Who can oppose him?
   He does anything he wants to do.
He carries out his plans against me.
   And he still has many other plans just like them.
That's why I'm so terrified.
   When I think about all of this, I'm afraid of him.
God has made my heart weak.
   The Mighty One has filled me with terror.

"Why doesn't the Mighty One set a time for judging sinful
    people?
  Why do those who know him have to keep waiting for that
    day?
People move their neighbor's boundary stones.
  They steal their neighbor's flocks.
The groans of those who are dying are heard from the city.
  Those who are wounded cry out for help.
  But God doesn't charge anyone with doing what is wrong.

"Who can prove that what I'm saying is wrong?
  Who can prove that my words aren't true?"

Then Bildad the Shuhite replied,

"God is King. He should be feared.
  He establishes peace in the highest parts of heaven.
How can human beings be right with God?
  How can mere people really be pure?
Even the moon isn't bright
  and the stars aren't pure in God's eyes.
So how about human beings? They are like maggots.
  How about mere people? They are like worms."

remember what you read

1. What is something you noticed for the first time?

That Bildad and Job's other friends only see God as far away. They don't see as their personal God.

2. What questions did you have?

None

3. Was there anything that bothered you?

No.

4. What did you learn about loving God?

That God is a God that is perfect and we should respect that and love him.

5. What did you learn about loving others?

If you have nothing comforting or nice to say don't say anything at all.

Job replied,

"Bildad, you haven't helped people who aren't strong!
　　You haven't saved people who are weak!
You haven't offered advice to those who aren't wise!
　　In fact, you haven't understood anything at all!
Who helped you say these things?
　　Whose spirit was speaking through you?

"God spreads out the northern skies over empty
　　　　space.
　　He hangs the earth over nothing.
He wraps up water in his clouds.
　　They are heavy, but they don't burst.
Those are only on the edges of what he does.
　　They are only the soft whispers that we hear from
　　　　him.
　　So who can understand how very powerful he is?"

"God hasn't treated me fairly.
　　The Mighty One has made my life bitter.
As long as I have life
　　and God gives me breath,
my mouth won't say evil things.
　　My lips won't tell lies.
I'll continue to say I'm right.
　　I'll never let go of that.
　　I won't blame myself as long as I live.

There are mines where silver is found.
  There are places where gold is purified.
Iron is taken out of the earth.
  Copper is melted down from ore.
Human beings light up the darkness.
  They search for ore in the deepest pits.
  They look for it in the blackest darkness.

But where can wisdom be found?
  Where does understanding live?
No human being understands how much it's worth.
  It can't be found anywhere in the world.

So where does wisdom come from?
  Where does understanding live?
It's hidden from the eyes of every living thing.
  Even the birds in the sky can't find it.
But God understands the way to it.
  He is the only one who knows where it lives.
He sees from one end of the earth to the other.
  He views everything in the world.
He made the mighty wind.
  He measured out the waters.
He gave orders for the rain to fall.
  He made paths for the thunderstorms.
Then he looked at wisdom and set its price.
  He established it and tested it.
He said to human beings,
  "Have respect for the Lord. That will prove you are wise.
  Avoid evil. That will show you have understanding."

Job continued to speak. He said,

"How I long for the times when things were better!
  That's when God watched over me.
The light of his lamp shone on me.
  I walked through darkness by his light.

Those were the best days of my life.
That's when God's friendship blessed my house.
The Mighty One was still with me.
My children were all around me.
The path in front of me was like sweet cream.
It was as if the rock poured out olive oil for me.

"But now those who are younger than I am make fun of me.
I wouldn't even put their parents with my sheep dogs!

"Now my life is slipping away.
Days of suffering grab hold of me.

"God, I cry out to you. But you don't answer me.
I stand up. But all you do is look at me.
You do mean things to me.
You attack me with your mighty power.

"I made an agreement with my eyes.
I promised not to look at a young woman with impure
thoughts.
What do we receive from God above?
What do we get from the Mighty One in heaven?
Sinful people are destroyed.
Trouble comes to those who do what is wrong.
Doesn't God see how I live?
Doesn't he count every step I take?

"I haven't told any lies.
My feet haven't hurried to cheat others.
So let God weigh me in honest scales.
Then he'll know I haven't done anything wrong.

"I wish someone would listen to me!
I'm signing my name to everything I've said.
I hope the Mighty One will give me his answer.
I hope the one who brings charges against me will write
them down."

The words of Job end here.

So the three men stopped answering Job, because he thought he was right. But Elihu the Buzite was very angry with Job. That's because Job said he himself was right instead of God. Elihu was the son of Barakel. He was from the family of Ram. Elihu was also very angry with Job's three friends. They hadn't found any way to prove that Job was wrong. But they still said he was guilty. Elihu had waited before he spoke to Job. That's because the others were older than he was. But he saw that the three men didn't have anything more to say. So he was very angry.

Elihu the Buzite, the son of Barakel, said,

"I'm young, and you are old.
   So I was afraid to tell you what I know.
I thought, 'Those who are older should speak first.
   Those who have lived for many years
      should teach people how to be wise.'

"Job, these men are afraid.
   They don't have anything else to say.
   They've run out of words.

"But I heard what you said.
   And here are the exact words I heard.
You said, 'I'm pure. I have done no wrong.
   I'm clean. I'm free from sin.
But God has found fault with me.
   He thinks I'm his enemy.
He puts my feet in chains.
   He watches every step I take.'

"But I'm telling you that you aren't right when you talk like
      that.
   After all, God is greater than any human being.
Why do you claim that God
   never answers anybody's questions?
He speaks in one way and then another.
   But we do not even realize it.

"Pay attention, Job! Listen to me!
    Be quiet so I can speak.
If you have anything to say, answer me.
    Speak up. I want to help you be cleared of all charges.
But if you don't have anything to say, listen to me.
    Be quiet so I can teach you how to be wise."

Elihu continued,

"Hear what I'm saying, you wise men.
    Listen to me, you who have learned so much.
Our tongues tell us what tastes good and what doesn't.
    And our ears tell us what's true and what isn't.
So let's choose for ourselves what is right.
    Let's learn together what is good.

"Job says, 'I'm not guilty of doing anything wrong.
    But God doesn't treat me fairly.'
Is there anyone like Job?
    He accuses God as easily as he drinks water.

"So listen to me, you men who have understanding.
    God would never do what is evil.
    The Mighty One would never do what is wrong.

"Job, if you have understanding, listen to me.
    Pay attention to what I'm saying.
Can someone who hates to be fair govern?
    Will you bring charges against the holy and mighty
        God?
He doesn't favor princes.
    He treats rich people and poor people the same.
    His hands created all of them.
They die suddenly in the middle of the night.
    God strikes them down, and they pass away.
    Even people who are mighty are removed, but not by
        human hands.

"Job, do you think it's fair for you to say,
    'I am the one who is right, not God'?

You ask him, 'What good is it for me not to sin?
  What do I get by not sinning?'

"I'd like to reply to you
  and to your friends who are with you.
Look up at the heavens.
  Observe the clouds that are high above you.
If you sin, what does that mean to God?
  If you sin many times, what does that do to him?
If you do what is right, how does that help him?
  What does he get from you?
The evil things you do only hurt people like yourself.
  The right things you do only help other human beings.

"Job, he wants to take you out of the jaws of trouble.
  He wants to bring you to a wide and safe place.
  He'd like to seat you at a table that is loaded with the best
    food.
But now you are loaded down
  with the punishment sinners will receive.
  You have been judged fairly.

"God is honored because he is so powerful.
  There is no teacher equal to him.

"When I hear the thunder, my heart pounds.
  It beats faster inside me.
Listen! Listen to the roar of his voice!
  Listen to the thunder that comes from him!

"Job, listen to me.
  Stop and think about the wonderful things God does.
Do you know how he controls the clouds?
  Do you understand how he makes his lightning flash?

"Job, tell us what we should say to God.
  We can't prepare our case
  because our minds are dark.
Out of the north, God comes in his shining glory.
  He comes in all his wonderful majesty.

We can't reach up to the Mighty One.
    He is lifted high because of his power.
Everything he does is fair and right.
    So he doesn't crush people.
That's why they have respect for him.
    He cares about all those who are wise."

remember what you read

1. What is something you noticed for the first time?

That Elihu has actually made a point
that God treats everyone fairly.

2. What questions did you have?

None.

3. Was there anything that bothered you?

No.

4. What did you learn about loving God?

That we shouldn't blame God for treating
us unfairly because God is fair and
we should respect him.

5. What did you learn about loving others?

That if we want to give a friend or
someone a present we should do it
because we want to.

JOB, PART 5

The LORD spoke to Job out of a storm. He said,

"Who do you think you are to disagree with my plans?
　You do not know what you are talking about.
Get ready to stand up for yourself.
　I will ask you some questions.
　Then I want you to answer me.

"Where were you when I laid the earth's foundation?
　Tell me, if you know.
Who measured it? I am sure you know!
　Who stretched a measuring line across it?
What was it built on?
　Who laid its most important stone?
When it happened, the morning stars sang together.
　All the angels shouted with joy.

"Who created the ocean?
　Who caused it to be born?
I put clouds over it as if they were its clothes.
　I wrapped it in thick darkness.
I set limits for it.
　I put its doors and metal bars in place.
I said, 'You can come this far.
　But you can't come any farther.
　Here is where your proud waves have to stop.'

"Job, have you ever commanded the morning to
　　come?
　Have you ever shown the sun where to rise?

The daylight takes the earth by its edges
   as if it were a blanket.
Then it shakes sinful people out of it.
The earth takes shape like clay stamped with an official's
     mark.
   Its features stand out
   like the different parts of your clothes.
Sinners would rather have darkness than light.
   When the light comes, their power is broken.

"Have you traveled to the springs at the bottom of the ocean?
   Have you walked in its deepest parts?
Have the gates of death been shown to you?
   Have you seen the gates of the deepest darkness?
Do you understand how big the earth is?
   Tell me, if you know all these things.

"Where does light come from?
   And where does darkness live?
Can you take them to their places?
   Do you know the paths to their houses?
I am sure you know! After all, you were already born!
   You have lived so many years!

"Have you entered the places where the snow is kept?
   Have you seen the storerooms for the hail?
I store up snow and hail for times of trouble.
   I keep them for days of war and battle.
Where does lightning come from?
   Where do the east winds live that blow across the earth?
Who tells the rain where it should fall?
   Who makes paths for the thunderstorms?
They bring water to places where no one lives.
   They water deserts that do not have anyone in them.

"Can you tie up the cords of the Pleiades?
   Can you untie the belt that Orion wears?
Can you bring out all the stars in their seasons?
   Can you lead out the Big Dipper and the Little Dipper?

Do you know the laws that govern the heavens?
　　Can you rule over the earth the way I do?

"Can you give orders to the clouds?
　　Can you make them pour rain down on you?
Do you send the lightning bolts on their way?
　　Do they report to you, 'Here we are'?

"Job, do you know when mountain goats have their
　　　　babies?
　　Do you watch when female deer give birth?
Do you count the months until the animals have their
　　　　babies?
　　Do you know the time when they give birth?
They bend their back legs and have their babies.
　　Then their labor pains stop.
Their little ones grow strong and healthy in the wild.
　　They leave and do not come home again.

"The wings of ostriches flap with joy.
　　But they can't compare with the wings and feathers
　　　　of storks.
Ostriches lay their eggs on the ground.
　　They let them get warm in the sand.
They do not know that something might step on
　　　　them.
　　A wild animal might walk all over them.
Ostriches are mean to their little ones.
　　They treat them as if they did not belong to them.
　　They do not care that their work was useless.
I did not provide ostriches with wisdom.
　　I did not give them good sense.
But when they spread their feathers to run,
　　they laugh at a horse and its rider.

"Job, do you give horses their strength?
　　Do you put flowing manes on their necks?
Do you make them jump like locusts?
　　They terrify others with their proud snorting.

They paw the ground wildly.
>They are filled with joy.
>They charge at their enemies.

"Job, are you wise enough to teach hawks where to fly?
>They spread their wings and fly toward the south.
Do you command eagles to fly so high?
>They build their nests as high as they can.
They live on cliffs and stay there at night.
>High up on the rocks they think they are safe.
From there they look for their food.
>They can see it from far away."

The LORD continued,

"I am the Mighty One.
>Will the man who argues with me correct me?
>Let him who brings charges against me answer me!"

Job replied to the LORD,

"I'm not worthy. How can I reply to you?
>I'm putting my hand over my mouth. I'll stop talking.
I spoke once. But I really don't have any answer.
>I spoke twice. But I won't say anything else."

Then the LORD spoke to Job out of the storm. He said,

"Get ready to stand up for yourself.
>I will ask you some more questions.
>Then I want you to answer me.

"Would you dare to claim that I am not being fair?
>Would you judge me in order to make yourself seem
>>right?
Is your arm as powerful as mine is?
>Can your voice thunder as mine does?
Then put on glory and beauty as if they were your clothes.
>Also put on honor and majesty.
Let loose your great anger.
>Look at those who are proud and bring them low.

Look at proud people and make them humble.
    Crush evil people right where they are.
Bury their bodies together in the dust.
    Cover their faces in the grave.
Then I myself will admit to you
    that your own right hand can save you.

Job replied to the LORD,

"I know that you can do anything.
    No one can keep you from doing what you plan to do.
You asked me, 'Who do you think you are to disagree with my
        plans?
    You do not know what you are talking about.'
I spoke about things I didn't completely understand.
    I talked about things that were too wonderful for me to
        know.

"You said, 'Listen now, and I will speak.
    I will ask you some questions.
    Then I want you to answer me.'
My ears had heard about you.
    But now my own eyes have seen you.
So I hate myself.
    I'm really sorry for what I said about you.
    That's why I'm sitting in dust and ashes."

After the LORD finished speaking to Job, he spoke to Eliphaz the
Temanite. He said, "I am angry with you and your two friends. You
have not said what is true about me, as my servant Job has. So now
get seven bulls and seven rams. Go to my servant Job. Then sacrifice a burnt offering for yourselves. My servant Job will pray for
you. And I will accept his prayer. I will not punish you for saying
the foolish things you said. You have not said what is true about
me, as my servant Job has." So Eliphaz the Temanite, Bildad the
Shuhite, and Zophar the Naamathite did what the LORD told them
to do. And the LORD accepted Job's prayer.

After Job had prayed for his friends, the LORD made him successful again. He gave him twice as much as he had before. All his brothers and sisters and everyone who had known him before came to see him. They ate with him in his house. They showed their concern for him. They comforted him because of all the troubles the LORD had brought on him. Each one gave him a piece of silver and a gold ring.

The LORD blessed the last part of Job's life even more than the first part. He gave Job 14,000 sheep and 6,000 camels. He gave him 1,000 pairs of oxen and 1,000 donkeys. Job also had seven sons and three daughters. He named the first daughter Jemimah. He named the second Keziah. And he named the third Keren-Happuch. Job's daughters were more beautiful than any other women in the whole land. Their father gave them a share of property along with their brothers.

After all of that happened, Job lived for 140 years. He saw his children, his grandchildren and his great-grandchildren. And so Job died. He had lived for a very long time.

remember what you read

1. What is something you noticed for the first time?

_____

_____

_____

_____

2. What questions did you have?

How old was Job when he died?

_____

_____

_____

3. Was there anything that bothered you?

No

_____

_____

_____

4. What did you learn about loving God?

That God corrects those he loves and we
should let God do that.

_____

_____

5. What did you learn about loving others?

That if we feel guilty about a conversation
or something you said to someone you
should apoligize to them and ask for
foregiveness.

introduction to Chronicles, parts 1-9

The books of 1 and 2 Chronicles, Ezra and Nehemiah are really one long story. Ezra and Nehemiah tell the story after the people of Judah return to Jerusalem from Babylon.

Chronicles–Ezra–Nehemiah tells how certain kings were faithful to take care of God's temple and worship him. The story tells only about kings who ruled in Jerusalem in Judah. The writer was not concerned about the northern kingdom of Israel, since God's temple was not there.

The first big section is a list of names called a genealogy. It gives all the details of how people were related. This allowed people to know who was supposed to be priests and work in the new temple. It also helped them know who had the right to be king in the renewed nation.

We begin reading the story just after Saul, the first king of Israel, and his sons were killed fighting the Philistines. His kingdom was given to David because Saul had disobeyed God.

The whole community of Israel came together to see David at Hebron. They said, "We are your own flesh and blood. In the past, Saul was our king. But you led the men of Israel in battle. The LORD your God said to you, 'You will be the shepherd over my people Israel. You will become their ruler.'"

All the elders of Israel came to see King David at Hebron. There he made a covenant with them in front of the LORD. They anointed David as king over Israel. It happened just as the LORD had promised through Samuel.

David and all the men of Israel marched to Jerusalem. But David captured the fort of Zion.

David had said, "Anyone who leads the attack against the Jebusites will become the commander of Israel's army." Joab went up first. So he became the commander of the army. He was the son of Zeruiah.

David moved into the fort. So it was called the City of David. He built up the city around the fort. He filled in the low places. He built a wall around it. During that time, Joab built up the rest of the city. David became more and more powerful. That's because the LORD who rules over all was with him.

The chiefs of David's mighty warriors and the whole community of Israel helped David greatly. They helped him become king over the entire land. That's exactly what the LORD had promised him. Here is a list of David's mighty warriors.

Jashobeam was chief of the officers. He was a Hakmonite. He used his spear against 300 men. He killed all of them at one time.

Next to him was Eleazar. He was one of the three mighty warriors. Jashobeam was with David at Pas Dammim. The Philistines had gathered there for battle. Israel's troops ran away from the Philistines. At the place where that happened, there was a field full of barley. The three mighty warriors took their stand in the middle of the field. They didn't let the Philistines capture it. They struck them down. The LORD helped them win a great battle.

David was near the rock at the cave of Adullam. Three of the 30 chiefs came down to him there. A group of Philistines was camped in the Valley of Rephaim. At that time David was in his usual place of safety. Some Philistine troops were stationed at Bethlehem. David really wanted some water. He said, "I wish someone would get me a drink of water from the well near the gate of Bethlehem!" So the three mighty warriors fought their way past the Philistine guards. They got some water from the well near the gate of Bethlehem. They took the water back to David. But David refused to drink it. Instead, he poured it out as a drink offering to the LORD. "I would never drink that water!"

David said. "It would be like drinking the blood of these men. They put their lives in danger by going to Bethlehem."

Those were some of the brave things the three mighty warriors did.

Abishai was chief over the three mighty warriors. He was the brother of Joab. Abishai used his spear against 300 men. He killed all of them. So he became as famous as the three mighty warriors. He was honored twice as much as the three mighty warriors. He became their commander. But he wasn't included among them.

Benaiah was a great hero from Kabzeel. He was the son of Jehoiada. Benaiah did many brave things. He struck down two of Moab's best fighting men. He also went down into a pit on a snowy day. He killed a lion there. And Benaiah struck down an Egyptian who was seven and a half feet tall. The Egyptian was holding a spear as big as a weaver's rod. Benaiah went out to fight against him with a club. He grabbed the spear out of the Egyptian's hand. Then he killed him with it. Those were some of the brave things Benaiah, the son of Jehoiada, did. He too was as famous as the three mighty warriors. He was honored more than any of the 30 chiefs. But he wasn't included among the three mighty warriors. And David put him in charge of his own personal guards.

There were also hundreds of soldiers who joined David when he was hiding from Saul. They agreed to make him king over all Israel. So David asked for their help moving the ark of God's covenant to Jerusalem.

David gathered together all the Israelites. They came to bring the ark of God from Kiriath Jearim to Jerusalem. The whole community of Israel went with him. All the people went there to get the ark of God the Lord. He sits on his throne between the cherubim. The ark is named after the Lord.

The ark of God was placed on a new cart. Then it was moved from Abinadab's house. Uzzah and Ahio were guiding it. David was celebrating with all his might in front of God. So was the whole community of Israel. All of them were singing songs.

They were also playing harps, lyres, tambourines, cymbals and trumpets.

They came to the threshing floor of Kidon. The oxen nearly fell there. So Uzzah reached out his hand to hold the ark steady. Then the LORD became very angry with Uzzah. The LORD struck him down because he had put his hand on the ark. So Uzzah died there in front of God.

David was afraid of God that day. David asked, "How can I ever bring the ark of God back here to me?" So he didn't take the ark to be with him in the City of David. Instead, he took it to the house of Obed-Edom. Obed-Edom was from Gath. The ark of God remained with the family of Obed-Edom. It stayed in his house for three months. And the LORD blessed his family. He also blessed everything that belonged to him.

The Philistines heard that David had been anointed king over the entire nation of Israel. So the whole Philistine army went to look for him. But David heard about it. He went out to where they were. The Philistines had come and attacked the people in the Valley of Rephaim. So David asked God for advice. David asked, "Should I go and attack the Philistines? Will you hand them over to me?"

The LORD answered him, "Go. I will hand them over to you."

So David and his men went up to Baal Perazim. There David won the battle over the Philistines. He said, "God has broken through against my enemies, just as water breaks through a dam." That's why the place was called Baal Perazim. The Philistines had left statues of their gods there. So David gave orders to burn them up.

Once more the Philistines attacked the people in the valley. So David asked God for advice again. God answered him, "Do not go straight after them. Instead, circle around them. Attack them in front of the poplar trees. Listen for the sound of marching in the tops of the trees. Then move out to fight. The sound will mean that I have gone out in front of you. I will strike down the Philistine army." So David did just as God had commanded him. He and his men struck down the Philistine army. They struck them down from Gibeon all the way to Gezer.

So David became famous in every land. The Lord made all the nations afraid of him.

David gathered the whole community of Israel together in Jerusalem. He wanted to carry up the ark of the Lord to the place he had prepared for it.

David sent for Zadok and Abiathar, the priests. He also sent for Uriel, Asaiah, Joel, Shemaiah, Eliel and Amminadab. They were Levites. He said to them, "You are the leaders of the families of Levi. You and the other Levites must set yourselves apart to serve the Lord and his people. You must carry up the ark of the Lord. He is the God of Israel. Put the ark in the place I've prepared for it. Remember when the anger of the Lord our God broke out against us? That's because it wasn't you Levites who tried to carry up the ark the first time. We didn't ask the Lord how to do it in the way the law requires." So the priests and Levites set themselves apart. Then they carried up the ark of the Lord. This time the Levites used the poles to carry on their shoulders the ark of God. That's what Moses had commanded in keeping with the word of the Lord.

David told the Levite leaders to appoint other Levites as musicians. He wanted them to make a joyful sound with lyres, harps and cymbals.

David and the elders of Israel went to carry up the ark of the covenant of the Lord. With great joy they carried up the ark from the house of Obed-Edom. God had helped the Levites who were carrying the ark of the covenant of the Lord. So seven bulls and seven rams were sacrificed. David was wearing a robe made out of fine linen. So were all the Levites who were carrying the ark. And so were the musicians and the choir director Kenaniah. David was also wearing a sacred linen apron. So the whole community of Israel brought up the ark of the covenant of the Lord. They shouted. They blew rams' horns and trumpets. They played cymbals, lyres and harps.

The ark of the covenant of the Lord was brought into the City of David. It was put in the tent David had set up for it. The priests brought burnt offerings and friendship offerings to God. After David finished sacrificing those offerings, he blessed the people in the name of the LORD. He gave to each Israelite man and woman a loaf of bread. He also gave each one a date cake and a raisin cake.

That day was the first time David appointed Asaph and his helpers. He appointed them to give praise to the LORD with these words.

Give praise to the LORD. Make his name known.
    Tell the nations what he has done.
Sing to him. Sing praise to him.
    Tell about all the wonderful things he has done.
Honor him, because his name is holy.
    Let the hearts of those who trust in the LORD be glad.
Look to the LORD and to his strength.
    Always look to him.
Remember the wonderful things he has done.
    Remember his miracles and how he judged our enemies.
Remember, you his servants, the children of Israel.
    Remember, you people of Jacob. Remember, you who are
        chosen by God.

He is the LORD our God.
    He judges the whole earth.
He will keep his covenant forever.
    He will keep his promise for all time to come.
He will keep the covenant he made with Abraham.
    He will keep the promise he made to Isaac.
He made it stand as a law for Jacob.
    He made it stand as a covenant for Israel. It will last forever.
He said, "I will give you the land of Canaan.
    It will belong to you."

Give thanks to the LORD, because he is good.
    His faithful love continues forever.

Then all the people said, "Amen!" They also said, "Praise the LORD."
    All the people left. Everyone went home. And David returned home to bless his family.

David moved into his palace. Then he spoke to Nathan the prophet. He said, "Here I am, living in a house that has beautiful cedar walls. But the ark of the covenant of the LORD is under a tent."

Nathan replied to David, "Do what you want to. God is with you."

remember what you read

1. What is something you noticed for the first time?

_____

_____

_____

_____

2. What questions did you have?

_____

_____

_____

_____

3. Was there anything that bothered you?

_____

_____

_____

_____

4. What did you learn about loving God?

_____

_____

_____

_____

5. What did you learn about loving others?

_____

_____

_____

_____

CHRONICLES, PART 2

God spoke to Nathan the prophet. He had him report to David that David would not build the house for God. But God would make David's son and many sons after them kings of Israel forever. And David's son would build God's house.

Then King David went into the holy tent. He sat down in front of the LORD. He said,

"LORD God, who am I? My family isn't important. So why have you brought me this far? I would have thought that you had already done more than enough for me. But now, my God, you have spoken about my royal house. You have said what will happen to it in days to come. LORD God, you have treated me as if I were the most honored man of all.

"LORD, there isn't anyone like you. There isn't any God but you. We have heard about it with our own ears. Who is like your people Israel? God, we are the one nation on earth you have saved. You have set us free for yourself. Your name has become famous. You have done great and wonderful things. You have driven out nations to make room for your people. You saved us when you set us free from Egypt. You made Israel your very own people forever. LORD, you have become our God.

"My God, you have shown me that you will build me a royal house. So I can pray to you boldly. You, LORD, are God! You have promised many good things to me. You have been pleased to bless my royal house. Now it will continue forever in your sight. LORD, you have blessed it. And it will be blessed forever."

While David was king of Israel, he won many battles over the Philistines. He brought them under his control. He took Gath away from the Philistines. He also captured the villages around Gath.

David also won the battle over the people of Moab. They were brought under his rule. They gave him the gifts he required them to bring him.

David fought against Hadadezer in the area of Hamath. Hadadezer was king of Zobah. He had gone to set up his monument at the Euphrates River. David captured 1,000 of Hadadezer's chariots, 7,000 chariot riders and 20,000 soldiers on foot. He cut the legs of all but 100 of the chariot horses.

The Arameans of Damascus came to help Hadadezer, the king of Zobah. But David struck down 22,000 of them. David stationed some soldiers in the Aramean kingdom of Damascus. The people of Aram were brought under his rule. They gave him the gifts he required them to bring him. The Lord helped David win his battles wherever he went.

Tou was king of Hamath. He heard that David had won the battle over the entire army of Hadadezer, the king of Zobah. So Tou sent his son Hadoram to King David. Hadoram greeted David. He praised him because David had won the battle over Hadadezer. Hadadezer had been at war with Tou. So Hadoram brought David all kinds of things made out of gold, of silver and of bronze.

King David set those things apart for the Lord. He had done the same thing with the silver and gold he had taken from other nations. The nations were Edom, Moab, Ammon, Philistia and Amalek.

Abishai struck down 18,000 men of Edom in the Valley of Salt. Abishai was the son of Zeruiah. Abishai stationed some soldiers in Edom. The whole nation of Edom was brought under his rule. The Lord helped David win his battles wherever he went.

David ruled over the whole nation of Israel. He did what was fair and right for all his people.

Joab, the son of Zeruiah, was commander over the army.
Jehoshaphat, the son of Ahilud, kept the records.
Zadok, the son of Ahitub, was a priest. Ahimelek, the son of Abiathar, was also a priest.
Shavsha was the secretary.

Benaiah, the son of Jehoiada, was commander over the Kereth-
ites and Pelethites.

And King David's sons were the chief officials who served at
his side.

*Many other nations were afraid of how powerful King David had
become. Sometimes they worked together to fight Israel. Sometimes
they fought against Israel alone. It didn't matter. God was with David
and the army of Israel. They took over the entire area God promised
to Abraham, even beyond the Euphrates River.*

Satan rose up against Israel. He stirred up David to count the
men of Israel. So David said to Joab and the commanders of the
troops, "Go! Count the men of Israel from Beersheba all the way
to Dan. Report back to me. Then I'll know how many there are."

Joab replied, "May the LORD multiply his troops 100 times. King
David, you are my master. Aren't all the men under your control?
Why would you want me to count them? Do you want to make
Israel guilty?"

In spite of what Joab said, the king's order had more authority than Joab's reply did. So Joab left and went all through Israel.
Then he came back to Jerusalem. Joab reported to David how
many fighting men he had counted. In the whole land of Israel
there were 1,100,000 men who could use their swords well. That
included 470,000 men in Judah.

But Joab didn't include the tribes of Levi and Benjamin in the
total number. The king's command was sickening to Joab. It was
also evil in the sight of God. So he punished Israel.

Then David said to God, "I committed a great sin when I counted
Israel's men. I beg you to take away my guilt. I've done a very foolish thing."

The LORD spoke to Gad, David's prophet. The LORD said, "Go and
tell David, 'The LORD says, "I could punish you in three different
ways. Choose one of them for me to punish you with."'"

So Gad went to David. Gad said to him, "The LORD says, 'Take
your choice. You can have three years when there will not be
enough food in the land. You can have three months when your

enemies will sweep you away. They will catch up with you. They will destroy you with their swords. Or you can have three days when the sword of the LORD will punish you. That means there would be three days of plague in the land. My angel would strike down people in every part of Israel.' So take your pick. Tell me how to answer the one who sent me."

David said to Gad, "I'm suffering terribly. Let me fall into the hands of the LORD. His mercy is very great. But don't let me fall into human hands."

So the LORD sent a plague on Israel. And 70,000 Israelites died. God sent an angel to destroy Jerusalem. But as the angel was doing it, the LORD saw it. The LORD decided to end the plague he had sent. So he spoke to the angel who was destroying the people. He said, "That is enough! Do not kill any more people!" The angel of the LORD was standing at Araunah's threshing floor. Araunah was from the city of Jebus.

David looked up. He saw the angel of the LORD standing between heaven and earth. The angel was holding out a sword over Jerusalem. David and the elders fell with their faces to the ground. They were wearing the rough clothing people wear when they're sad.

David said to God, "I ordered the fighting men to be counted. I'm the one who has sinned. I am the shepherd of these people. I'm the one who has done what is wrong. These people are like sheep. What have they done? LORD my God, punish me and my family. But don't let this plague continue to strike your people."

Then the angel of the LORD ordered Gad to tell David to go up to the threshing floor of Araunah, the Jebusite. He wanted David to build an altar there to honor the LORD. So David went up and did it. He obeyed the message that Gad had spoken in the LORD's name.

David bought Araunah's property and sacrificed offerings to God. God told the angel to put his sword away.

David announced, "The house of the LORD God will be built here. Israel's altar for burnt offerings will also be here."

Then he sent for his son Solomon. He told him to build a house for the LORD, the God of Israel. David said to Solomon, "My son, with all my heart I wanted to build a house for the LORD my God. That's where his Name will be. But a message from the LORD came to me. It said, 'You have spilled the blood of many people. You have fought many wars. You are not the one who will build a house for my Name. That is because I have seen you spill the blood of many people on the earth. But you are going to have a son. He will be a man of peace. And I will give him peace and rest from all his enemies on every side. His name will be Solomon. I will give Israel peace and quiet while he is king. He will build a house for my Name. He will be my son. And I will be his father. I will make his kingdom secure over Israel. It will last forever.'

"My son, may the LORD be with you. May you have success. May you build the house of the LORD your God, just as he said you would. May the LORD give you good sense. May he give you understanding when he makes you king over Israel. Then you will keep the law of the LORD your God. Be careful to obey the rules and laws the LORD gave Moses for Israel. Then you will have success. Be strong and brave. Don't be afraid. Don't lose hope.

"I've tried very hard to provide for the LORD's temple. I've provided 3,750 tons of gold and 37,500 tons of silver. I've provided more bronze and iron than anyone can weigh. I've also given plenty of wood and stone. You can add to it. You have a lot of workers. You have people who can cut stones and people who can lay the stones. You have people who can work with wood. You also have people who are skilled in every other kind of work. Some of them can work with gold and silver. Others can work with bronze and iron. There are more workers than anyone can count. So begin the work. May the LORD be with you."

Then David ordered all Israel's leaders to help his son Solomon. He said to them, "The LORD your God is with you. He's given you peace and rest on every side. He's handed over to me the people who are living in the land. The land has been brought under the control of the LORD and his people. So be committed to the LORD your God with all your heart and soul. Start building the temple of the LORD God. Then bring the ark of the covenant of the LORD into it. Also bring in the sacred objects that belong to God. The temple will be built for the Name of the LORD."

remember what you read

1. What is something you noticed for the first time?

_____

_____

_____

_____

2. What questions did you have?

_____

_____

_____

_____

3. Was there anything that bothered you?

_____

_____

_____

_____

4. What did you learn about loving God?

_____

_____

_____

_____

5. What did you learn about loving others?

_____

_____

_____

_____

David had become very old. So he made his son Solomon king over Israel.

David praised the LORD in front of the whole community. He said,

"LORD, we give you praise.
  You are the God of our father Israel.
  We give you praise for ever and ever.
LORD, you are great and powerful.
  Glory, majesty and beauty belong to you.
  Everything in heaven and on earth belongs to you.
LORD, the kingdom belongs to you.
  You are honored as the one who rules over all.
Wealth and honor come from you.
  You are the ruler of all things.
In your hands are strength and power.
  You can give honor and strength to everyone.
Our God, we give you thanks.
  We praise your glorious name.

"But who am I? And who are my people? Without your help we wouldn't be able to give this much. Everything comes from you. We've given back to you only what comes from you."

The next day they offered sacrifices to the LORD. They brought burnt offerings to him. They sacrificed 1,000 bulls, 1,000 rams and 1,000 male lambs. They also brought the required drink offerings. And they offered many other sacrifices for the whole community of Israel. They ate and drank with great joy that day. They did it in front of the LORD. Then they announced a second time that Solomon was king. He was the son of David. They anointed Solomon in front of the LORD. They anointed him to be ruler. They also anointed Zadok to be priest.

So Solomon sat on the throne of the LORD. He ruled as king in place of his father David. Things went well with him. All the people of Israel obeyed him. All the officers and warriors promised to be completely faithful to King Solomon. So did all of King David's sons.

The LORD greatly honored Solomon in the sight of all the people. He gave him royal majesty. Solomon was given more glory than any king over Israel ever had before.

David was king over the whole nation of Israel. He was the son of Jesse. He ruled over Israel for 40 years. He ruled for seven years in Hebron and for 33 years in Jerusalem. He died when he was very old. He had enjoyed a long life. He had enjoyed wealth and honor. David's son Solomon became the next king after him.

∽≬≬∾

Solomon was the son of David. Solomon made his position secure over his kingdom. The LORD his God was with him. He made Solomon very great.

Solomon and the people of Israel went to Gibeon. They worshiped God there at God's tent Moses had made after the Israelites came out of Egypt.

That night God appeared to Solomon. He said to him, "Ask for anything you want me to give you."

Solomon answered God, "You were very kind to my father David. Now you have made me king in his place. LORD God, let the promise you gave to my father David come true. You have made me king. My people are as many as the dust of the earth. They can't be counted. Give me wisdom and knowledge. Then I'll be able to lead these people. Without your help, who would be able to rule this great nation of yours?"

God said to Solomon, "I am glad that those are the things you really want. You have not asked for wealth, possessions or honor. You have not even asked to have your enemies killed. You have not asked to live for a long time. Instead, you have asked for wisdom and knowledge. You want to be able to rule my people wisely. I have made you king over them. So wisdom and knowledge will be given to you. I will also give you wealth, possessions and honor. You will have more than any king before you ever had. And no king after you will have as much."

Then Solomon left the high place at Gibeon. He went from the tent of meeting there to Jerusalem. And he ruled over Israel.

Solomon ordered that God's temple and his palace be built. He worked with Hiram, the king of Tyre to the north of Israel. Hiram provided wood for the temple and workers with all the skills needed to make beautiful buildings.

Then Solomon began to build the temple of the LORD. He built it on Mount Moriah in Jerusalem. That's where the LORD had appeared to Solomon's father David. The LORD had appeared at the threshing floor of Araunah. Solomon began building the temple on the second day of the second month. It was in the fourth year of his rule.

Solomon laid the foundation for God's temple. It was 90 feet long and 30 feet wide. Solomon's men followed the standard measure used at that time. The porch in front of the temple was 30 feet across and 30 feet high.

Solomon covered the inside of the temple with pure gold. He covered the inside of the main hall with juniper boards. Then he covered the boards with fine gold. He decorated the hall with palm tree patterns and chain patterns. He decorated the temple with valuable jewels. The gold he used came from Parvaim. He covered the ceiling beams, doorframes, walls and doors of the temple with gold. He carved cherubim on the walls.

He built the Most Holy Room. It was as long as the temple was wide. It was 30 feet long and 30 feet wide. He covered the inside of the Most Holy Room with 23 tons of fine gold. He also covered the upper parts with gold. The gold on the nails weighed 20 ounces.

For the Most Holy Room, Solomon made a pair of carved cherubim. He covered them with gold. The total length of the cherubim's wings from tip to tip was 30 feet. One wing of the first cherub was seven and a half feet long. Its tip touched the temple wall. The other wing was also seven and a half feet long. Its tip touched the wing tip of the other cherub. In the same way one wing of the second cherub was seven and a half feet long. Its tip touched the other temple wall. The other wing was also seven and a half feet long. Its tip touched the wing tip of the first cherub. So the total length of the wings of the two cherubim was 30 feet from tip to tip. The cherubim stood facing the main hall.

So Huram finished the work he had started for King Solomon. Here's what he made for God's temple.

He made the two pillars.

He made the two tops for the pillars. The tops were shaped like bowls.

He made the two sets of chains that were linked together. They decorated the two bowl-shaped tops of the pillars.

He made the 400 pomegranates for the two sets of chains. There were two rows of pomegranates for each chain. They decorated the bowl-shaped tops of the pillars.

He made the stands and their bowls.

He made the huge bowl. He made the 12 bulls that were under it.

He made the pots, shovels and meat forks. He also made all the things used with them.

Huram-Abi made all these objects for King Solomon for the LORD's temple. He made them out of bronze. There were too many of them to weigh. In fact, it was impossible to add up the weight of all the bronze.

Solomon also made all the objects that were in God's temple.

He made the golden altar.

He made the tables for the holy bread.

He made the pure gold lampstands and their lamps. The lamps burned in front of the Most Holy Room, just as the law required.

He made the gold flowers. He made the gold lamps and tongs. They were made out of solid gold.

He made the wick cutters, sprinkling bowls, dishes, and shallow cups for burning incense. All of them were made out of pure gold. He made the gold doors of the temple. They were the inner doors to the Most Holy Room and the doors of the main hall.

Solomon finished all the work for the LORD's temple. Then he brought in the things his father David had set apart for the LORD. They included the silver and gold and all the objects for God's temple. Solomon placed them there with the other treasures.

Then Solomon sent for the elders of Israel. He told them to come to Jerusalem. All the Israelites came together to where the king was. It was at the time of the Feast of Booths. The feast was held in the seventh month.

The priests brought the ark of the LORD's covenant to its place in the Most Holy Room of the temple. They put it under the wings of the cherubim. The cherubim's wings were spread out over the place where the ark was. They covered the ark. They also covered the poles used to carry it.

Then a cloud filled the temple of the LORD. The priests couldn't do their work. That's because the cloud of the LORD's glory filled God's temple.

Then Solomon said, "LORD, you have said you would live in a dark cloud. I've built a beautiful temple for you. You can live in it forever.

"LORD, you are the God of Israel. There is no God like you in heaven or on earth. You keep the covenant you made with us. You show us your love. You do that when we follow you with all our hearts. You have kept your promise to my father David. He was your servant. With your mouth you made a promise. With your powerful hand you have made it come true. And today we can see it.

"But will God really live on earth with human beings? After all, the heavens can't hold you. In fact, even the highest heavens can't hold you. So this temple I've built certainly can't hold you! But please pay attention to my prayer. Lord my God, be ready to help me as I make my appeal to you. Listen to my cry for help. Hear the prayer I'm praying to you. Let your eyes look toward this temple day and night. You said you would put your Name here. Listen to the prayer I'm praying toward this place. Hear me when I ask you to help us. Listen to your people Israel when they pray toward this place. Listen to us from heaven. It's the place where you live. When you hear us, forgive us.

Solomon continued praying a long prayer. He asked God to forgive Israel when they did not keep the covenant agreement. He asked God to show himself to people who came from far away to worship him. He asked God to always provide for his people and forgive them.

"My God, let your eyes see us. Let your ears pay attention to the prayers offered in this place.

"Lord God, rise up and come to your resting place.
　Come in together with the ark.
　It's the sign of your power.
Lord God, may your priests put on salvation as if it were
　their clothes.
　May your faithful people be glad because you are so good.
Lord God, don't turn your back on your anointed king.
　Remember the great love you promised to your servant
　David."

Solomon finished praying. Then fire came down from heaven. It burned up the burnt offering and the sacrifices. The glory of the Lord filled the temple. The priests couldn't enter the temple of the Lord because his glory filled it. All the Israelites saw the fire coming down. They saw the glory of the Lord above the temple. So they got down on their knees in the courtyard with their faces toward the ground. They worshiped the Lord. They gave thanks to him and said,

"The Lord is good.
　His faithful love continues forever."

remember what you read

1. What is something you noticed for the first time?

_____

_____

_____

_____

2. What questions did you have?

_____

_____

_____

_____

3. Was there anything that bothered you?

_____

_____

_____

_____

4. What did you learn about loving God?

_____

_____

_____

_____

5. What did you learn about loving others?

_____

_____

_____

_____

Solomon finished the LORD's temple and the royal palace. He had done everything he had planned to do in the LORD's temple and his own palace. The LORD appeared to him at night. The LORD said,

"I have heard your prayer. I have chosen this place for myself. It is a temple where sacrifices will be offered.

"Suppose I close up the sky and there isn't any rain. Suppose I command locusts to eat up the crops. And I send a plague among my people. But they make themselves humble in my sight. They pray and look to me. And they turn from their evil ways. Then I will listen to them from heaven. I will forgive their sin. And I will heal their land. After all, they are my people. Now my eyes will see them. My ears will pay attention to the prayers they offer in this place. I have chosen this temple. I have set it apart for myself. My Name will be there forever. My eyes and my heart will always be there.

"But you must walk faithfully with me, just as your father David did. Do everything I command you to do. Obey my rules and laws. Then I will set up your royal throne. I made a covenant with your father David to do that. I said to him, 'You will always have a son from your family line to rule over Israel.'

"But suppose all of you turn away from me. You refuse to obey the rules and commands I have given you. And you go off to serve other gods and worship them. Then I will remove Israel from my land. It is the land I gave them. I will turn my back on this temple. I will do it even though I have set it apart for my Name to be there. I will make all the nations hate it.

They will laugh and joke about it. This temple will become a pile of stones. All those who pass by it will be shocked. They will say, 'Why has the LORD done a thing like this to this land and temple?' People will answer, 'Because they have deserted the LORD. He is the God of their people who lived long ago. He brought them out of Egypt. But they have been holding on to other gods. They've been worshiping them. They've been serving them. That's why the LORD has brought all this horrible trouble on them.'"

The queen of Sheba heard about how famous Solomon was. So she came to Jerusalem to test him with hard questions. She could hardly believe everything she had seen. She gave the king four and a half tons of gold. She also gave him huge amounts of spices and valuable jewels. There had never been as many spices as the queen of Sheba gave to King Solomon.

Each year Solomon received 25 tons of gold. That didn't include the money brought in by business and trade. All the kings of Arabia also brought gold and silver to Solomon. So did the governors of the territories.

King Solomon was richer than all the other kings on earth. He was also wiser than they were. All these kings wanted to meet Solomon in person. They wanted to see for themselves how wise God had made him. Year after year, everyone who came to him brought a gift. They brought gifts made out of silver and gold. They brought robes, weapons and spices. They also brought horses and mules.

The other events of Solomon's rule from beginning to end are written down. They are written in the records of Nathan the prophet. They are written in the prophecy of Ahijah. He was from Shiloh. They are also written in the records of the visions of Iddo the prophet about Jeroboam. Jeroboam was the son of Nebat. Solomon ruled in Jerusalem over the whole nation of Israel for 40 years. Then he joined the members of his family who had already died. He was buried in the city of his father David. Solomon's son Rehoboam became the next king after him.

Rehoboam went to the city of Shechem. All the Israelites had gone there to make him king. Jeroboam heard about it. He was the son of Nebat. Jeroboam was in Egypt at that time. He had gone there for safety. He wanted to get away from King Solomon. But now he returned from Egypt. So the people sent for Jeroboam. He and all the people went to Rehoboam. They said to him, "Your father put a heavy load on our shoulders. But now make our hard work easier. Make the heavy load on us lighter. Then we'll serve you."

Rehoboam answered, "Come back to me in three days." So the people went away.

Then King Rehoboam asked the elders for advice. They had served his father Solomon while he was still living. Rehoboam asked them, "What advice can you give me? How should I answer these people?"

They replied, "Be kind to them. Please them. Give them what they are asking for. Then they'll always serve you."

But Rehoboam didn't accept the advice the elders gave him. He asked for advice from the young men who had grown up with him and were now serving him. He asked them, "What's your advice? How should I answer these people? They said to me, 'Make the load your father put on our shoulders lighter.' "

The young men who had grown up with him gave their answer. They replied, "The people have said to you, 'Your father put a heavy load on our shoulders. Make it lighter.' Now tell them, 'My little finger is stronger than my father's legs. My father put a heavy load on your shoulders. But I'll make it even heavier. My father beat you with whips. But I'll beat you with bigger whips.' "

Three days later Jeroboam and all the people returned to Rehoboam. That's because the king had said, "Come back to me in three days." The king answered them in a mean way. He didn't accept the advice of the elders. Instead, he followed the advice of the young men. He said, "My father put a heavy load on your shoulders. But I'll make it even heavier. My father beat you with whips. But I'll beat you with bigger whips." So the king didn't listen to the people. That's because God had planned it that way. What the LORD had said through Ahijah came true. Ahijah had spoken the LORD's message to Jeroboam, the son of Nebat. Ahijah was from Shiloh.

All the Israelites saw that the king refused to listen to them. So they answered the king. They said,

"We don't have any share in David's royal family.
    We don't have any share in Jesse's son.
People of Israel, let's go back to our homes.
    David's royal family, take care of your own kingdom!"

So all the Israelites went home. But Rehoboam still ruled over the Israelites who were living in the towns of Judah.

Rehoboam had made his position as king secure. He had become very strong. Then he turned away from the law of the Lord. So did all the people of Judah. They hadn't been faithful to the Lord. So Shishak attacked Jerusalem. It was in the fifth year that Rehoboam was king. Shishak was king of Egypt. He came with 1,200 chariots and 60,000 horsemen. Troops of Libyans, Sukkites and Cushites came with him from Egypt. There were so many of them they couldn't be counted. Shishak captured the cities of Judah that had high walls around them. He came all the way to Jerusalem.

Then Shemaiah the prophet came to Rehoboam and the leaders of Judah. They had gathered together in Jerusalem. They were afraid of Shishak. Shemaiah said to them, "The Lord says, 'You have left me. So now I am leaving you to Shishak.'"

The king and the leaders of Israel made themselves humble in the Lord's sight. They said, "The Lord does what is right and fair."

The Lord saw they had made themselves humble. So he gave a message to Shemaiah. The Lord said, "They have made themselves humble in my sight. So I will not destroy them. Instead, I will soon save them. Even though I am very angry with Jerusalem, I will not use Shishak to destroy them. But the people of Jerusalem will be brought under his control. Then they will learn the difference between serving me and serving the kings of other lands."

Shishak, the king of Egypt, attacked Jerusalem. He carried away the treasures of the Lord's temple. He also carried the treasures of the royal palace away. He took everything.

Rehoboam had made himself humble in the Lord's sight. So the Lord turned his anger away from him. Rehoboam wasn't totally destroyed. In fact, some good things happened in Judah.

King Rehoboam had made his position secure in Jerusalem. He continued as king. He was 41 years old when he became king. He ruled for 17 years in Jerusalem. It was the city the LORD had chosen out of all the cities in the tribes of Israel. He wanted to put his Name there. The name of Rehoboam's mother was Naamah from Ammon. Rehoboam did what was evil. That's because he hadn't worshiped the LORD with all his heart.

The events of Rehoboam's rule from beginning to end are written down. They are written in the records of Shemaiah and Iddo, the prophets. The records deal with family histories. Rehoboam and Jeroboam were always at war with each other. Rehoboam joined the members of his family who had already died. He was buried in the City of David. Rehoboam's son Abijah became the next king after him.

ᕱᏯᏯᏯᕽ

Abijah became king of Judah. It was in the 18th year of Jeroboam's rule over Israel. Abijah ruled in Jerusalem for three years. His mother's name was Maakah. She was a daughter of Uriel. Uriel was from Gibeah.

There was war between Abijah and Jeroboam. Abijah went into battle with an army of 400,000 capable fighting men. Jeroboam lined up his soldiers against them. He had 800,000 able troops.

Abijah stood on Mount Zemaraim. It's in the hill country of Ephraim. Abijah said, "Jeroboam and all you Israelites, listen to me! The LORD is the God of Israel. Don't you know that he has placed David and his sons after him on Israel's throne forever? People of Israel, don't fight against the LORD. He's the God of your people who lived long ago. You can't possibly succeed."

Jeroboam had sent some troops behind Judah's battle lines. He told them to hide and wait there. He and his men stayed in front of Judah's lines. Judah turned and saw that they were being attacked from the front and from the back. Then they cried out to the LORD. The priests blew their trumpets. The men of Judah shouted the battle cry. When they did, God drove Jeroboam and all the Israelites away from Abijah and Judah. The Israelites ran away from them. God handed Israel over to Judah. Abijah and his troops wounded and killed large numbers of them. In fact, 500,000 of Israel's capable men lay dead or wounded. So at that time the Israelites were brought under Judah's control. The people of Judah won the battle over them. That's because they trusted in the LORD, the God of their people.

But Abijah grew stronger. The other events of Abijah's rule are written down. The things he did and said are written in the notes of Iddo the prophet.

Abijah joined the members of his family who had already died. He was buried in the City of David. Abijah's son Asa became the next king after him. While Asa was king, the country had peace and rest for ten years.

remember what you read

1. What is something you noticed for the first time?

_____

_____

_____

_____

2. What questions did you have?

_____

_____

_____

_____

3. Was there anything that bothered you?

_____

_____

_____

_____

4. What did you learn about loving God?

_____

_____

_____

_____

5. What did you learn about loving others?

_____

_____

_____

_____

CHRONICLES, PART 5

༄

Asa did what was good and right in the eyes of the LORD his God. Asa removed the altars where false gods were worshiped. He commanded Judah to worship the LORD, the God of their people. He commanded them to obey the LORD's laws and commands. Asa removed the high places and incense altars from every town in Judah. The kingdom had peace and rest under his rule. He built up the cities of Judah that had high walls around them. The land was at peace. No one was at war with Asa during those years. That's because the LORD gave him peace and rest.

Asa had an army of 300,000 men from Judah. They carried spears and large shields. There were 280,000 men from Benjamin. They were armed with bows and small shields. All these men were brave soldiers.

Zerah marched out against them. He was from Cush. He had a huge army of thousands. He also had 300 chariots. They came all the way to Mareshah. Asa went out to meet Zerah in battle. They took up their positions in the Valley of Zephathah. It's near Mareshah.

Then Asa called out to the LORD his God. He said, "LORD, there isn't anyone like you. You help the weak against the strong. LORD our God, help us. We trust in you. In your name we have come out to fight against this huge army. LORD, you are our God. Don't let mere human beings win the battle over you."

The LORD struck down the men of Cush for Asa and Judah. The Cushites ran away. Asa and his army chased them all the way to

Gerar. A large number of Cushites fell down wounded or dead. So they couldn't fight back. The LORD and his army crushed them. The men of Judah carried off a large amount of goods. They destroyed all the villages around Gerar. The LORD had made the people in those villages afraid of him. The men of Judah took everything from all the villages. They also attacked the camps of those who took care of the herds. They carried off large numbers of sheep, goats and camels. Then they returned to Jerusalem.

The Spirit of God came on Azariah. He was the son of Oded. Azariah went out to meet Asa. He said to him, "Asa and all you people of Judah and Benjamin, listen to me. The LORD is with you when you are with him. If you really look for him, you will find him. But if you desert him, he will desert you. For a long time Israel didn't worship the true God. They didn't have a priest who taught them. So they didn't know God's law. But when they were in trouble, they turned to the LORD, the God of Israel. When they did, they found him. In those days it wasn't safe to travel around. The people who lived in all the areas of the land were having a lot of trouble. One nation was crushing another. One city was crushing another. That's because God was causing them to suffer terribly. But be strong. Don't give up. God will reward you for your work."

Asa heard that prophecy. He paid attention to the words of Azariah the prophet, the son of Oded. So Asa became bolder than ever. He removed the statues of gods from the whole land of Judah and Benjamin. He also removed them from the towns he had captured in the hills of Ephraim. He did it because the LORD hated those gods. Asa repaired the altar of the LORD. It was in front of the porch of the LORD's temple.

There weren't any more wars until the 35th year of Asa's rule.

When Asa trusted and worshiped God, God protected Judah. Later, Asa asked the king of Aram for help in a battle. Because he didn't trust God, he had to fight wars for the rest of his life.

The events of Asa's rule from beginning to end are written down. They are written in the records of the kings of Judah and Israel. In the 39th year of Asa's rule his feet began to hurt. The pain was terrible. But even though he was suffering, he didn't look to the LORD for help. All he did was go to the doctors. In the 41st year of Asa's rule he joined the members of his family who had already died. He was buried in a tomb. He had cut it out for himself in the City of David. His body was laid on a wooden frame. It was covered with spices and different mixes of perfume. A huge fire was made to honor him.

Jehoshaphat was the son of Asa. Jehoshaphat became the next king after him. He made his kingdom strong in case Israel would attack him. He placed troops in all the cities of Judah that had high walls around them. He stationed some soldiers in Judah. He also put some in the towns of Ephraim that his father Asa had captured.

The LORD was with Jehoshaphat. That's because he lived the way King David had lived. He didn't ask for advice from the gods that were named Baal. Instead, Jehoshaphat obeyed the God of his father. He obeyed the LORD's commands instead of the practices of Israel. The LORD made the kingdom secure under Jehoshaphat's control. All the people of Judah brought gifts to Jehoshaphat. So he had great wealth and honor. His heart was committed to living the way the LORD wanted him to. He removed the high places from Judah. He also removed the poles used to worship the female god named Asherah.

In the third year of his rule, he sent his officials to teach in the towns of Judah. They took the Book of the Law of the LORD with them. They went around to all the towns of Judah. And they taught the people.

All the kingdoms of the lands around Judah became afraid of the LORD. So they didn't go to war against Jehoshaphat. Some Philistines brought to Jehoshaphat the gifts and silver he required of them. The Arabs brought him their flocks. They brought him 7,700 rams and 7,700 goats.

After that, the Moabites, Ammonites and some Meunites went to war against Jehoshaphat.

Some people came and told him, "A huge army is coming from Edom to fight against you." Jehoshaphat was alarmed. So he decided to ask the Lord for advice. He told all the people of Judah to go without eating. The people came together to ask the Lord for help. In fact, they came from every town in Judah to pray to him.

Then Jehoshaphat stood up among the people of Judah and Jerusalem. He was in front of the new courtyard at the Lord's temple. He said,

"Lord, you are the God of our people who lived long ago. You are the God who is in heaven. You rule over all the kingdoms of the nations. You are strong and powerful. No one can fight against you and win. Our God, you drove out the people who lived in this land. You drove them out to make room for your people Israel. You gave this land forever to those who belong to the family line of your friend Abraham. They have lived in this land. They've built a temple here for your Name. They have said, 'Suppose trouble comes on us. It doesn't matter whether it's a punishing sword, or plague or hunger. We'll serve you. We'll stand in front of this temple where your Name is. We'll cry out to you when we're in trouble. Then you will hear us. You will save us.'

"But here are men from Ammon, Moab and Mount Seir. You wouldn't allow Israel to march in and attack their territory when the Israelites came from Egypt. So Israel turned away from them. They didn't destroy them. See how they are paying us back. They are coming to drive us out. They want to take over the land you gave us as our share. Our God, won't you please judge them? We don't have the power to face this huge army that's attacking us. We don't know what to do. But we're looking to you to help us."

All the men of Judah stood there in front of the Lord. Their wives, children and little ones were with them.

Jehoshaphat bowed down with his face toward the ground. All the people of Judah and Jerusalem also bowed down. They worshiped the Lord. Then some Levites from the families of Kohath and Korah stood up. They praised the Lord, the God of Israel. They praised him with very loud voices.

Early in the morning all the people left for the Desert of Tekoa. As they started out, Jehoshaphat stood up. He said, "Judah, listen to me! People of Jerusalem, listen to me! Have faith in the LORD your God. He'll take good care of you. Have faith in his prophets. Then you will have success." Jehoshaphat asked the people for advice. Then he appointed men to sing to the LORD. He wanted them to praise the LORD because of his glory and holiness. They marched out in front of the army. They said,

"Give thanks to the LORD.
    His faithful love continues forever."

They began to sing and praise him. Then the LORD hid some men and told them to wait. He wanted them to attack the people of Ammon, Moab and Mount Seir. They had gone into Judah and attacked it. But they lost the battle. The Ammonites and Moabites rose up against the men from Mount Seir. They destroyed them. They put an end to them. When they finished killing the men from Seir, they destroyed one another.

The men of Judah came to the place that looks out over the desert. They turned to look down at the huge army. But all they saw was dead bodies lying there on the ground. No one had escaped. So Jehoshaphat and his men went down there to carry off anything of value. Among the dead bodies they found a large amount of supplies, clothes and other things of value. There was more than they could take away. There was so much it took three days to collect all of it. There they praised the LORD.

Then all the men of Judah and Jerusalem returned to Jerusalem. They were filled with joy. Jehoshaphat led them. The LORD had made them happy because all their enemies were dead. They entered Jerusalem and went to the LORD's temple. They were playing harps, lyres and trumpets.

All the surrounding kingdoms began to have respect for God. They had heard how the LORD had fought against Israel's enemies. The kingdom of Jehoshaphat was at peace. His God had given him peace and rest on every side.

So Jehoshaphat ruled over Judah. He was 35 years old when he became Judah's king. He ruled in Jerusalem for 25 years. His mother's name was Azubah. She was the daughter of Shilhi. Jehoshaphat followed the ways of his father Asa. He didn't wander away from them. He did what was right in the eyes of the LORD. But the high places weren't removed. The people still hadn't worshiped the God of Israel with all their hearts.

The other events of Jehoshaphat's rule from beginning to end are written down. They are written in the official records of Jehu, the son of Hanani. They are written in the records of the kings of Israel.

Jehoshaphat joined the members of his family who had already died. He was buried in the family tomb in the City of David. Jehoshaphat's son Jehoram became the next king after him.

remember what you read

1. What is something you noticed for the first time?

_____

_____

_____

_____

2. What questions did you have?

_____

_____

_____

_____

3. Was there anything that bothered you?

_____

_____

_____

_____

4. What did you learn about loving God?

_____

_____

_____

_____

5. What did you learn about loving others?

_____

_____

_____

_____

Jehoram made his position secure over his father's kingdom. Then he killed all his brothers with his sword. He also killed some of the officials of Israel. Jehoram was 32 years old when he became king. He ruled in Jerusalem for eight years. He followed the ways of the kings of Israel, just as the royal family of Ahab had done. In fact, he married a daughter of Ahab. Jehoram did what was evil in the eyes of the LORD. But the LORD didn't want to destroy the royal family of David. That's because the LORD had made a covenant with him. The LORD had promised to keep the lamp of David's kingdom burning brightly forever.

Jehoram received a letter from Elijah the prophet. In it, Elijah said,

> "The LORD is the God of your father David. The LORD says, 'You have not followed the ways of your own father Jehoshaphat or of Asa, the king of Judah. Instead, you have followed the ways of the kings of Israel. You have led Judah and the people of Jerusalem to worship other gods, just as the royal family of Ahab did. Also, you have murdered your own brothers. They were members of your own family. They were better men than you are. So now the LORD is about to strike down your people with a heavy blow. He will strike down your sons, your wives and everything that belongs to you. And you yourself will be very sick for a long time. The sickness will finally cause your insides to come out.'"

After all of that, the LORD made Jehoram very sick. He couldn't be healed. After he had been sick for two years, the sickness caused his insides to come out. He died in great pain. His people didn't make a funeral fire to honor him. They had made funeral fires to honor the kings who ruled before him.

Jehoram was 32 years old when he became king. He ruled in Jerusalem for eight years. No one was sorry when he passed away. He was buried in the City of David. But he wasn't placed in the tombs of the kings.

ૠૠ

The people of Jerusalem made Ahaziah king in place of Jehoram. Ahaziah was 22 years old when he became king. He ruled in Jerusalem for one year. His mother's name was Athaliah. She was a granddaughter of Omri.

Ahaziah also followed the ways of the royal family of Ahab. That's because Ahaziah's mother gave him bad advice. So he did what was evil in the eyes of the Lord. He did what the family of Ahab had done.

Ahaziah visited King Joram of Israel. God told an army commander named Jehu to destroy the whole family of Ahab. So he killed Joram and Ahaziah.

ૠૠ

Athaliah was Ahaziah's mother. She saw that her son was dead. So she began to wipe out the whole royal family of Judah. But Jehosheba went and got Joash, the son of Ahaziah. Jehosheba was the daughter of King Jehoram. She stole Joash away from among the royal princes. All of them were about to be murdered. She put Joash and his nurse in a bedroom. Jehosheba, the daughter of King Jehoram, was the wife of Jehoiada the priest. She was also Ahaziah's sister. So Jehosheba hid the child from Athaliah. That's why Athaliah couldn't kill him. The child remained hidden with the priest and his wife at God's temple for six years. Athaliah ruled over the land during that time.

When Joash was seven years old, Jehoiada showed how strong

he was. He made a covenant with the commanders of groups of 100 men. They went all through Judah. They gathered together the Levites and the leaders of Israelite families from all the towns. They came to Jerusalem. The whole community made a covenant with the new king at God's temple.

Jehoiada said to them, "Ahaziah's son will rule over Judah. That's what the LORD promised concerning the family line of David."

Jehoiada and his sons brought Ahaziah's son out. They put the crown on him. They gave him a copy of the covenant. And they announced that he was king. They anointed him. Then they shouted, "May the king live a long time!"

Athaliah heard the noise of the people running and cheering the new king. So she went to them at the LORD's temple. She looked, and there was the king! He was standing next to his pillar at the entrance. The officers and trumpet players were standing beside the king. All the people of the land were filled with joy. They were blowing trumpets. Musicians with their musical instruments were leading the songs of praise. Then Athaliah tore her royal robes. She shouted, "Treason! It's treason!"

Jehoiada the priest sent out the commanders of the groups of 100 men. They were in charge of the troops. He said to them, "Bring her away from the temple between the line of guards. Use your swords to kill anyone who follows her." The priest had said, "Don't put her to death at the LORD's temple." So they grabbed her as she reached the entrance of the Horse Gate on the palace grounds. There they put her to death.

Then Jehoiada made a covenant. He promised that he, the people and the king would be the LORD's people. All the people went to Baal's temple. They tore it down. They smashed the altars and the statues of gods. They killed Mattan in front of the altars. He was the priest of Baal.

Joash was seven years old when he became king. He ruled in Jerusalem for 40 years. His mother's name was Zibiah. She was from Beersheba. Joash did what was right in the eyes of the LORD. Joash lived that way as long as Jehoiada the priest was alive.

Some time later Joash decided to make the LORD's temple look like new again. He called together the priests and Levites. He said to them, "Go to the towns of Judah. Collect the money that the nation of Israel owes every year. Use it to repair the temple of your God. Do it now."

The men in charge of the work did their best. The repairs went very well under them. They rebuilt God's temple. They did it in keeping with its original plans. They made the temple even stronger. So they finished the work. As long as Jehoiada lived, burnt offerings were sacrificed continually at the LORD's temple.

After Jehoiada died, the officials of Judah came to King Joash. They bowed down to him. He listened to them. They turned their backs on the temple of the LORD, the God of their people. They worshiped poles made to honor the female god named Asherah. They also worshiped statues of other gods. Because Judah and Jerusalem were guilty of sin, God became angry with them. The LORD sent prophets to the people to bring them back to him. The prophets told the people what they were doing wrong. But the people wouldn't listen.

Then the Spirit of God came on Zechariah the priest. He was the son of Jehoiada. Zechariah stood in front of the people. He told them, "God says, 'Why do you refuse to obey my commands? You will not have success. You have deserted me. So I have deserted you.'"

In the spring, the army of Aram marched into Judah and Jerusalem against Joash. They killed all the leaders of the people. They took a large amount of goods from Judah. They sent it to their king in Damascus. The army of Aram had come with only a few men. But the LORD allowed them to win the battle over a much larger army. Judah had deserted the LORD, the God of their people. That's why the LORD punished Joash. The army of Aram pulled back. They left Joash badly wounded. His officials planned to do evil things to him. That's because he murdered the son of Jehoiada the priest. They killed Joash in his bed. So he died.

The story of the sons of Joash is written in the notes on the records of the kings. The many prophecies about him are written there too. So is the record of how he made God's temple look like new again. Joash's son Amaziah became the next king after him.

Amaziah was 25 years old when he became king. He ruled in Jerusalem for 29 years. His mother's name was Jehoaddan. She was from Jerusalem. Amaziah did what was right in the eyes of the LORD. But he didn't do it with all his heart. The kingdom was firmly under his control. So he put to death the officials who had murdered his father, the king.

Then Amaziah showed how strong he was. He led his army to the Valley of Salt. There he killed 10,000 men of Seir. The army of Judah also captured 10,000 men alive. The army of Judah took them to the top of a cliff. Then they threw them down. All of them were smashed to pieces.

Amaziah returned from killing the men of Edom. He brought back the statues of the gods of Seir. He set them up as his own gods. He bowed down to them. He burned sacrifices to them. The LORD was very angry with Amaziah. He sent a prophet to him. The prophet said, "Why do you ask the gods of those people for advice? They couldn't even save their own people from your power!"

While the prophet was still speaking, the king spoke to him. He said, "Did I ask you for advice? Stop! If you don't, you will be struck down."

So the prophet stopped. But then he said, "I know that God has decided to destroy you. That's because you have worshiped other gods. You haven't listened to my advice."

Amaziah, the king of Judah, spoke to his advisers. Then he sent a message to Jehoash, the king of Israel. Amaziah dared Jehoash, "Come on! Let us face each other in battle!"

But Jehoash, the king of Israel, answered Amaziah, the king of Judah. Jehoash said, "You brag that you have won the battle over Edom. You are very proud. But stay home! Why ask for trouble? Why bring yourself crashing down? Why bring Judah down with you?"

But Amaziah wouldn't listen. That's because God had planned to hand Judah over to Jehoash. After all, they had asked the gods of Edom for advice. So Jehoash, the king of Israel, attacked. He and Amaziah, the king of Judah, faced each other in battle. Israel drove

Judah away. Every man ran home. Jehoash king of Israel captured Amaziah king of Judah at Beth Shemesh. Jehoash brought Amaziah to Jerusalem. Jehoash broke down part of its wall. It's the part that went from the Ephraim Gate to the Corner Gate. That part of the wall was 600 feet long. Jehoash took all the gold and silver. He took all the objects he found in God's temple. Obed-Edom had been in charge of them. Jehoash also took the palace treasures and the prisoners. Then he returned to Samaria.

Amaziah king of Judah lived for 15 years after Jehoash king of Israel died. The other events of Amaziah's rule from beginning to end are written down. They are written in the records of the kings of Judah and Israel. Amaziah turned away from obeying the LORD. From that time on, some people made evil plans against him in Jerusalem. So he ran away to Lachish. But they sent men after him to Lachish. There they killed him.

All the people of Judah made Uzziah king. He was 16 years old. They made him king in place of his father Amaziah.

remember what you read

1. What is something you noticed for the first time?

_____

_____

_____

_____

2. What questions did you have?

_____

_____

_____

_____

3. Was there anything that bothered you?

_____

_____

_____

_____

4. What did you learn about loving God?

_____

_____

_____

_____

5. What did you learn about loving others?

_____

_____

_____

_____

Uzziah was 16 years old when he became king. He ruled in Jerusalem for 52 years. His mother's name was Jekoliah. She was from Jerusalem. Uzziah did what was right in the eyes of the LORD, just as his father Amaziah had done. He tried to obey God during the days of Zechariah. Zechariah taught him to have respect for God. As long as Uzziah obeyed the LORD, God gave him success.

Uzziah went to war against the Philistines. He broke down the walls of Gath, Jabneh and Ashdod. Then he rebuilt some towns that were near Ashdod. He also rebuilt some other towns where Philistines lived. God helped him fight against the Philistines. He also helped him fight against the Meunites and against the Arabs who lived in Gur Baal. The Ammonites brought to Uzziah the gifts he required of them. He became famous all the way to the border of Egypt. That's because he had become very powerful.

But after Uzziah became powerful, his pride brought him down. He wasn't faithful to the LORD his God. He entered the LORD's temple to burn incense on the altar for burning incense. Azariah the priest followed him in. So did 80 other brave priests of the LORD. They stood up to Uzziah. They said, "Uzziah, it isn't right for you to burn incense to the LORD. Only the priests are supposed to do that. They are members of the family line of Aaron. They have been set apart to burn incense. So get out of here. Leave the temple. You haven't been faithful. The LORD God won't honor you."

Uzziah was holding a shallow cup. He was ready to burn incense in it. He became angry. He shouted at the priests in the LORD's temple. He did it near the altar for burning incense. While he was shouting, a skin disease suddenly broke out on his forehead. Azariah the chief priest and all the other priests looked at him. They saw that Uzziah had a skin disease on his forehead. So they hurried him out of the temple. Actually, he himself really wanted to leave. He knew that the LORD was making him suffer.

King Uzziah had the skin disease until the day he died. He lived in a separate house because he had the disease. And he wasn't allowed to enter the LORD's temple. Uzziah's son Jotham was in charge of the palace. Jotham ruled over the people of the land.

The other events of Uzziah's rule from beginning to end were written down by Isaiah the prophet. Isaiah was the son of Amoz. Uzziah joined the members of his family who had already died. He was buried near them in a royal burial ground. People said, "He had a skin disease." Uzziah's son Jotham became the next king after him.

⁓᷈᷈᷈᷈᷈᷈᷈⁓

Jotham was 25 years old when he became king. He ruled in Jerusalem for 16 years. His mother's name was Jerusha. She was the daughter of Zadok. Jotham did what was right in the eyes of the LORD, just as his father Uzziah had done. But Jotham didn't enter the LORD's temple as Uzziah had done. The people, however, continued to do very sinful things. Jotham rebuilt the Upper Gate of the LORD's temple. He did a lot of work on the wall at the hill of Ophel. He built towns in the hill country of Judah. He also built forts and towers in areas that had a lot of trees in them.

Jotham became powerful. That's because he had worshiped the LORD his God with all his heart.

The other events of Jotham's rule are written down. That includes all his wars and the other things he did. All these things are written in the records of the kings of Israel and Judah. Jotham was 25 years old when he became king. He ruled in Jerusalem for 16 years. Jotham joined the members of his family who had already died. He was buried in the City of David. Jotham's son Ahaz became the next king after him.

Ahaz was 20 years old when he became king. He ruled in Jerusalem for 16 years. He didn't do what was right in the eyes of the LORD. He didn't do what King David had done. He followed the ways of the kings of Israel. He also made statues of gods that were named Baal. He burned sacrifices in the Valley of Ben Hinnom. He sacrificed his children in the fire to other gods. He followed the practices of the nations. The LORD hates these practices. The LORD had driven out those nations to make room for the people of Israel. Ahaz offered sacrifices and burned incense at the high places. He also did it on the tops of hills and under every green tree.

So the LORD his God handed him over to the king of Aram. The men of Aram won the battle over him. They took many of his people as prisoners. They brought them to Damascus.

When King Ahaz was in trouble, he became even more unfaithful to the LORD. Ahaz offered sacrifices to the gods of Damascus. They had won the battle over him. Ahaz thought, "The gods of the kings of Aram have helped them. So I'll sacrifice to those gods. Then they'll help me." But those gods only caused his ruin. In fact, those gods caused the ruin of the whole nation of Israel.

Ahaz gathered together everything that belonged to God's temple. He cut all of it in pieces. Ahaz shut the doors of the LORD's temple. He set up altars at every street corner in Jerusalem. In every town in Judah he built high places. Sacrifices were burned there to other gods. That made the LORD, the God of his people, very angry.

The other events of the rule of Ahaz and all his evil practices from beginning to end are written down. They are written in the records of the kings of Judah and Israel. Ahaz joined the members of his family who had already died. He was buried in the city of Jerusalem. But he wasn't placed in the tombs of the kings of Israel. Ahaz's son Hezekiah became the next king after him.

Hezekiah was 25 years old when he became king. He ruled in Jerusalem for 29 years. His mother's name was Abijah. She was the daughter of Zechariah. Hezekiah did what was right in the eyes of the LORD, just as King David had done.

In the first month of Hezekiah's first year as king, he opened the doors of the LORD's temple. He repaired them. He brought the priests and Levites in. He said, "Levites, listen to me! Set yourselves apart to the LORD. Set apart the temple of the LORD. He's the God of your people who lived long ago. Remove anything 'unclean' from the temple. Our people weren't faithful. They did what was evil in the eyes of the LORD our God. So the LORD has become angry with Judah and Jerusalem. He has made them look so bad that everyone is shocked when they see them. They laugh at them. You can see it with your own eyes. That's why our fathers have been killed by swords. That's why our sons and daughters and wives have become prisoners. So I'm planning to make a covenant with the LORD, the God of Israel. Then he'll stop being angry with us. My sons, don't fail to obey the LORD. He has chosen you to stand in front of him and work for him. He wants you to serve him and burn incense to him."

All these Levites went to King Hezekiah. They reported, "We've purified the whole temple of the LORD. That includes the altar for burnt offerings and all its tools. It also includes the table for the holy bread and all its objects. We've prepared all the things King Ahaz had removed. We've set them apart to the LORD. Ahaz had removed them while he was king. He wasn't faithful to the LORD. Those things are now in front of the LORD's altar."

King Hezekiah led all the people in sacrificing many animals to the true God of Israel. He had musicians play to praise God. The priests began the regular work in the temple that Ahaz had stopped. Hezekiah and all the people worshiped God with joy. Hezekiah also sent a letter to all the people telling them to celebrate the Passover Feast:

"People of Israel, return to the LORD. He is the God of Abraham, Isaac and Israel. Return to him. Then he will return to you who are left in the land. You have escaped from the power of the kings of Assyria. Don't be like your parents and the rest of your people. They weren't faithful to the LORD, the God of their people. That's why he punished them. He made them look so bad that everyone was shocked when they saw them. You can see it for yourselves. Don't be stubborn. Don't be as your people were. Obey the LORD. Come to his temple. He has set it apart to himself forever. Serve the LORD your God. Then he'll stop being angry with you. Suppose you return to the LORD. Then those who captured your relatives and children will be kind to them. In fact, your relatives and children will come back to this land. The LORD your God is kind and tender. He won't turn away from you if you return to him."

A very large crowd of people gathered together in Jerusalem. They went there to celebrate the Feast of Unleavened Bread. It took place in the second month. They removed the altars in Jerusalem. They cleared away the altars for burning incense. They threw all the altars into the Kidron Valley.

They killed the Passover lamb on the 14th day of the second month. The priests and Levites were ashamed of how they had lived. They set themselves apart to the LORD. They brought burnt offerings to his temple. Then they did their regular tasks just as the Law of Moses, the man of God, required.

The people of Israel who were in Jerusalem celebrated the Feast of Unleavened Bread. They celebrated for seven days with great joy.

Hezekiah spoke words that gave hope to all the Levites. They understood how to serve the LORD well. For the seven days of the feast they ate the share given to them. They also sacrificed friendship offerings. They praised the LORD, the God of their people.

Then the whole community agreed to celebrate the feast for seven more days. So for another seven days they celebrated with joy. The priests and Levites gave their blessing to the people. God heard them. Their prayer reached all the way to heaven. It's the holy place where God lives.

The Passover Feast came to an end. The people of Israel who

were in Jerusalem went out to the towns of Judah. They smashed the sacred stones. They cut down the poles used to worship the female god named Asherah. They destroyed the high places and the altars. They did those things all through Judah and Benjamin. They also did them in Ephraim and Manasseh. They destroyed all the objects used to worship other gods. Then the Israelites returned to their own towns and property.

Hezekiah did what was good and right. He was faithful to the LORD his God. He tried to obey his God. He worked for him with all his heart. That's the way he worked in everything he did to serve God's temple. He obeyed the law. He followed the LORD's commands. So he had success.

Sennacherib, king of Assyria, marched into Judah. He wanted to take all the cities for himself. But Hezekiah told the people to trust God. The Assyrians came to Jerusalem and made fun of Israel's God. They wanted to take control of Jerusalem.

remember what you read

1. What is something you noticed for the first time?

_____

_____

_____

_____

2. What questions did you have?

_____

_____

_____

_____

3. Was there anything that bothered you?

_____

_____

_____

_____

4. What did you learn about loving God?

_____

_____

_____

_____

5. What did you learn about loving others?

_____

_____

_____

_____

CHRONICLES, PART 8

King Hezekiah cried out in prayer to God in heaven. He prayed about the problem Jerusalem was facing. So did Isaiah the prophet. The Lord sent an angel. The angel wiped out all the enemy's fighting men, commanders and officers. He put an end to them right there in the camp of the Assyrian king. So Sennacherib went back to his own land in shame. He went into the temple of his god. There some of his own sons, the people closest to him, killed him with their swords.

So the Lord saved Hezekiah and the people of Jerusalem. He saved them from the power of Sennacherib, the king of Assyria. He also saved them from all their other enemies. He took care of them on every side. Many people brought offerings to Jerusalem for the Lord. They brought expensive gifts for Hezekiah, the king of Judah. From then on, all the nations thought well of him.

In those days Hezekiah became sick. He knew he was about to die. So he prayed to the Lord. And the Lord answered him. He gave him a miraculous sign. But Hezekiah's heart was proud. He didn't give thanks for the many kind things the Lord had done for him. So the Lord became angry with him. He also became angry with Judah and Jerusalem. Then Hezekiah had a change of heart. He was sorry he had been proud. The people of Jerusalem were also sorry they had sinned. So the Lord wasn't angry with them as long as Hezekiah was king.

Hezekiah was very rich. He received great honor. He made storerooms for his silver and gold. He also made them for his jewels, spices, shields and all kinds of expensive things. He made buildings to store the harvest of grain, fresh wine and olive oil. He made barns for all kinds of cattle. He made sheep pens for his flocks. He built villages. He gained large numbers of flocks and herds. God had made him very rich.

Hezekiah did many things that showed he was faithful to the Lord. Those things and the other events of his rule are written down. They are written in the record of the vision of the prophet Isaiah, the son of Amoz. That record is part of the records of the kings of Judah and Israel. Hezekiah joined the members of his family who had already died. He was buried on the hill where the tombs of David's family are. The whole nation of Judah honored him when he died. So did the people of Jerusalem. Hezekiah's son Manasseh became the next king after him.

⟡⟡⟡

Manasseh was 12 years old when he became king. He ruled in Jerusalem for 55 years. Manasseh did what was evil in the eyes of the Lord. He followed the practices of the nations. The Lord hated those practices. Manasseh rebuilt the high places. His father Hezekiah had destroyed them. Manasseh also set up altars to the gods that were named Baal. He made poles used to worship the female god named Asherah. He even bowed down to all the stars and worshiped them. He built altars in the Lord's temple. The Lord had said about his temple, "My Name will remain in Jerusalem forever." In the two courtyards of the Lord's temple Manasseh built altars to honor all the stars in the sky. He sacrificed his children in the fire to other gods. He did it in the Valley of Ben Hinnom. He practiced all kinds of evil magic. He took part in worshiping evil powers. He got messages from people who had died. He talked to the spirits of people who have died. He did many things that were evil in the eyes of the Lord. Manasseh made the Lord very angry.

Manasseh had carved a statue of a god. He put it in God's temple. Manasseh led Judah and the people of Jerusalem astray. They did more evil things than the nations the Lord had destroyed to make room for the Israelites.

The Lord spoke to Manasseh and his people. But they didn't pay any attention to him. So the Lord brought the army commanders of the king of Assyria against them. They took Manasseh as a prisoner. They put a hook in his nose. They put him in bronze chains. And they took him to Babylon. When Manasseh was in trouble, he asked the Lord his God to help him. He made himself very humble in the sight of the God of his people. Manasseh prayed to him. When he did, the Lord felt sorry for him. He answered his prayer. The Lord brought Manasseh back to Jerusalem and his kingdom. Then Manasseh knew that the Lord is God.

Manasseh got rid of the false gods. He removed the statue of one of those gods from the Lord's temple. He also removed all the altars he had built on the temple hill and in Jerusalem. He threw them out of the city. Then he made the Lord's altar look like new again. He sacrificed friendship offerings and thank offerings on it. He told the people of Judah to serve the Lord, the God of Israel. The people continued to offer sacrifices at the high places. But they offered them only to the Lord their God.

The other events of Manasseh's rule are written down in the official records of the kings of Judah. Manasseh joined the members of his family who had already died. He was buried in his palace. Manasseh's son Amon became the next king after him.

∽✷✷✷✷∾

Amon was 22 years old when he became king. He ruled in Jerusalem for two years. Amon did what was evil in the eyes of the Lord, just as his father Manasseh had done. Amon worshiped and offered sacrifices to all the statues of gods that Manasseh had made. He didn't make himself humble in the Lord's sight as his father Manasseh had done. So Amon became even more guilty.

Amon's officials made plans against him. They murdered him in his palace. Then the people of the land killed all those who had made plans against King Amon. They made his son Josiah king in his place.

∽✷✷✷✷∾

Josiah was eight years old when he became king. He ruled in Jerusalem for 31 years. He did what was right in the eyes of the

LORD. He lived the way King David had lived. He didn't turn away from it to the right or the left.

While he was still young, he began to worship the God of King David. It was the eighth year of Josiah's rule. In his 12th year Josiah began to get rid of the high places in Judah and Jerusalem. He removed the poles used to worship the female god named Asherah. He also removed the statues of other false gods. He ordered the altars of the gods that were named Baal to be torn down. Josiah cut to pieces the altars above them that were used for burning incense. He smashed the Asherah poles. He also smashed the statues of other false gods. Josiah broke all of them to pieces. He scattered the pieces over the graves of those who had offered sacrifices to those gods. He burned the bones of the priests on their altars. That's the way he made Judah and Jerusalem pure and "clean." Josiah went to the towns of Manasseh, Ephraim and Simeon. He went all the way to Naphtali. He also went to the destroyed places around all those towns. Everywhere Josiah went he tore down the altars and the Asherah poles. He crushed the statues of gods to powder. He cut to pieces all the altars for burning incense. He destroyed all those things everywhere in Israel. Then he went back to Jerusalem.

In the 18th year of Josiah's rule, he decided to make the land and temple pure and "clean." So he sent Shaphan, Maaseiah and Joah to repair the temple of the LORD his God.

These men went to Hilkiah the high priest. They gave him the money that had been brought into God's temple. The Levites who guarded the gates had collected it. They had received some of the money from the people of Manasseh and Ephraim. They had also received some from the other people who remained in Israel. The rest of the money came from other people. It came from all the people of Judah and Benjamin and the people living in Jerusalem. Men were appointed to direct the work on the LORD's temple. All the money collected was given to them. These men paid the workers who repaired the temple. They made it look like new again. They also gave money to the builders and those who worked with wood. The workers used it to buy lumber and blocks of stone. The lumber was used for the supports and beams for the buildings. The kings of Judah had let the buildings fall down.

At that time Hilkiah the priest found the Book of the Law of the LORD. It had been given through Moses. Hilkiah spoke to Shaphan the secretary. Hilkiah said, "I've found the Book of the Law in the LORD's temple." Hilkiah gave the book to Shaphan.

Then Shaphan took the book to King Josiah. He told him, "Your officials are doing everything they've been asked to do. They have paid out the money that was in the LORD's temple. They've put it in the care of the directors and workers." Shaphan continued, "Hilkiah the priest has given me a book." Shaphan read some of it to the king.

The king heard the words of the Law. When he did, he tore his royal robes. He gave orders to Hilkiah, Ahikam, Abdon, Shaphan the secretary and Asaiah. Josiah commanded them, "Go. Ask the LORD for advice. Ask him about what is written in this book that has been found. Do it for me. Also do it for the people who remain in Israel and Judah. The LORD has been very angry with us. That's because our people before us didn't obey what the LORD had said. They didn't do everything written in this book."

Hilkiah and the people the king had sent with him went to speak to Huldah the prophet. Huldah lived in the New Quarter of Jerusalem.

Huldah said to them, "The LORD is the God of Israel. He says, 'Here is what you should tell the man who sent you to me. "The LORD says, 'I am going to bring horrible trouble on this place and its people. There are curses written down in the book that has been read to the king of Judah. All those curses will take place. That's because the people have deserted me. They have burned incense to other gods. They have made me very angry because of everything their hands have made. So my anger will burn like a fire against this place. And the fire of my anger will not be put out.' "' The king of Judah sent you to ask for advice. Tell him, 'The LORD is the God of Israel. He has a message for you about the things you heard. The LORD says, "Your heart was tender. You made yourself humble in my sight. You heard what I spoke against this place and its people. So you made yourself humble. You tore your royal robes and wept. And I have heard you," announces the LORD. You will join the members of your family who have already died. You will be buried in peace. You will not see all the trouble I am going to bring. I am going to bring trouble on this place and the people who live here.'"

Huldah's answer was taken back to the king.

remember what you read

1. What is something you noticed for the first time?

_____

_____

_____

_____

2. What questions did you have?

_____

_____

_____

_____

3. Was there anything that bothered you?

_____

_____

_____

_____

4. What did you learn about loving God?

_____

_____

_____

_____

5. What did you learn about loving others?

_____

_____

_____

_____

Then the king called together all the elders of Judah and Jerusalem. He went up to the LORD's temple. The people of Judah and Jerusalem went with him. So did the priests and Levites. All of them went, from the least important of them to the most important. The king had all the words of the Book of the Covenant read to them. The book had been found in the LORD's temple. The king stood next to his pillar. He agreed to the terms of the covenant in front of the LORD. The king promised to serve the LORD and obey his commands, directions and rules. He promised to obey them with all his heart and with all his soul. So the king promised to obey the terms of the covenant that were written in that book.

Then he had everyone in Jerusalem and in Benjamin commit themselves to the covenant. The people of Jerusalem did it in keeping with the covenant of the God of Israel.

Josiah removed all the statues of false gods from the whole territory that belonged to the Israelites. The LORD hated those statues. Josiah had everyone in Israel serve the LORD their God. As long as he lived, they didn't fail to follow the LORD, the God of their people.

Josiah celebrated the Passover Feast in Jerusalem to honor the LORD. The Passover lamb was killed on the 14th day of the first month. Josiah appointed the priests to their duties. He cheered them up as they served the LORD at his temple. The Levites taught all the people of Israel. The Levites had been set apart to the LORD.

Josiah provided animals for the Passover offerings. He gave them for all the people who were there. He gave a total of 30,000 lambs and goats and 3,000 oxen. He gave all of them from his own possessions.

So at that time the entire service to honor the LORD was carried out. The Passover Feast was celebrated. The burnt offerings were sacrificed on the LORD's altar. That's what King Josiah had ordered. The Israelites who were there celebrated the Passover Feast at that time. They observed the Feast of Unleavened Bread for seven days. The Passover Feast hadn't been observed like that in Israel since the days of Samuel the prophet. None of the kings of Israel had ever celebrated a Passover Feast like Josiah's. He celebrated it with the priests and Levites. All the people of Judah and Israel were there along with the people of Jerusalem. He celebrated it with them too. That Passover Feast was celebrated in the 18th year of Josiah's rule.

Josiah had put the temple in order. After all of that, Necho went up to fight at Carchemish. He was king of Egypt. Carchemish was on the Euphrates River. Josiah marched out to meet Necho in battle. But Necho sent messengers to him. They said, "Josiah king of Judah, there isn't any trouble between you and me. I'm not attacking you at this time. I'm at war with another country. God told me to hurry. He's with me. So stop opposing him. If you don't, he'll destroy you."

But Josiah wouldn't turn away from Necho. Josiah wore different clothes so people wouldn't recognize him. He wanted to go to war against Necho. He wouldn't listen to what God had commanded Necho to say. Instead, Josiah went out to fight him on the plains of Megiddo.

Men who had bows shot arrows at King Josiah. After he was hit, he told his officers, "Take me away. I'm badly wounded." So they took him out of his chariot. They put him in his other chariot. They brought him to Jerusalem. There he died. He was buried in the tombs of his family. All the people of Judah and Jerusalem mourned for him.

Josiah did many things that showed he was faithful to the LORD. Those things and the other events of Josiah's rule were in keeping with what is written in the Law of the LORD. All the events from beginning to end are written down. They are written in the records of the kings of Israel and Judah.

The people of the land went and got Jehoahaz. He was the son of Josiah. The people made Jehoahaz king in Jerusalem in place of his father.

⤲⤳

Jehoahaz was 23 years old when he became king. He ruled in Jerusalem for three months. The king of Egypt removed him from his throne in Jerusalem. Necho, the king of Egypt, made Eliakim king over Judah and Jerusalem. Eliakim was a brother of Jehoahaz. Necho changed Eliakim's name to Jehoiakim. But Necho took Eliakim's brother Jehoahaz with him to Egypt.

⤲⤳

Jehoiakim was 25 years old when he became king. He ruled in Jerusalem for 11 years. He did what was evil in the eyes of the LORD his God. Nebuchadnezzar attacked him. Nebuchadnezzar was king of Babylon. He put Jehoiakim in bronze chains. And he took him to Babylon. Nebuchadnezzar also took to Babylon objects from the LORD's temple. He put them in his own temple there.

The other events of Jehoiakim's rule are written in the records of the kings of Israel and Judah. He did things the LORD hated. Those things and everything that happened to him are also written in those records. Jehoiakim's son Jehoiachin became the next king after him.

⤲⤳

Jehoiachin was 18 years old when he became king. He ruled in Jerusalem for three months and ten days. He did what was evil in the eyes of the LORD. In the spring, King Nebuchadnezzar sent for him. He brought him to Babylon. He also brought things of value from the LORD's temple. He made Zedekiah king over Judah and Jerusalem. Zedekiah was Jehoiachin's uncle.

⤲⤳

Zedekiah was 21 years old when he became king. He ruled in Jerusalem for 11 years. He did what was evil in the eyes of the LORD his God. He didn't pay any attention to the message the LORD spoke through Jeremiah the prophet. Zedekiah also refused to remain under the control of King Nebuchadnezzar. The king had forced Zedekiah to make a promise in God's name. But Zedekiah's heart became very stubborn. He wouldn't turn to the LORD, the God of Israel. And that's not all. The people and all the leaders of the priests became more and more unfaithful. They followed all the practices of the nations. The LORD hated those practices. The people and leaders made the LORD's temple "unclean." The LORD had set the temple in Jerusalem apart in a special way for himself.

The LORD, the God of Israel, sent word to his people through his messengers. He sent it to them again and again. He took pity on his people. He also took pity on the temple where he lived. But God's people made fun of his messengers. They hated his words. They laughed at his prophets. Finally the LORD's great anger was stirred up against his people. Nothing could save them. The LORD brought the king of the Babylonians against them. The Babylonian army killed their young people with their swords at the temple. They didn't spare young men or young women. They didn't spare the old people or weak people either. God handed all of them over to Nebuchadnezzar. Nebuchadnezzar carried off to Babylon all the objects from God's temple. Some of those things were large. Others were small. He carried off the treasures of the temple. He also carried off the treasures that belonged to the king and his officials. The Babylonians set God's temple on fire. They broke down the wall of Jerusalem. They burned all the palaces. They destroyed everything of value there.

Nebuchadnezzar took the rest of the people to Babylon as prisoners. They had escaped from being killed by swords. They served him and those who ruled after him. That lasted until the kingdom of Persia came to power. The land of Israel enjoyed its sabbath years. It rested. That deserted land wasn't farmed for a full 70 years. What the LORD had spoken through Jeremiah came true.

introduction to Ezra and Nehemiah

Cyrus, king of Persia, gave an order to the Jews who wanted to return to Jerusalem. He told them to go back and rebuild the temple. After the temple was built, King Artaxerxes sent Ezra to Jerusalem. Ezra needed to make sure everyone was following God's law correctly. Ezra was a priest. He was part of the family of Aaron, the brother of Moses and the first priest of Israel.

Nehemiah served King Artaxerxes. The king sent him back to Jerusalem to rebuild the wall around the city. Nehemiah and Ezra worked together to make sure the people were living as God's people should.

ᴄᴐᴼᴼᴼ

It was the first year of the rule of Cyrus. He was king of Persia. The Lord inspired him to send a message all through his kingdom. It happened so that what the Lord had spoken through Jeremiah would come true. The message was written down. It said,

"Cyrus, the king of Persia, says,

" 'The Lord is the God of heaven. He has given me all the kingdoms on earth. He has appointed me to build a temple for him at Jerusalem in Judah. Any of his people among you may go up to Jerusalem and build the Lord's temple. He is the God of Israel. He is the God who is in Jerusalem. And may their God be with them. The people still left alive in every place must bring gifts to the people going. They must provide silver and gold to the people going up to Jerusalem. The people must bring goods and livestock. They should also bring any offerings they choose to. All those gifts will be for God's temple in Jerusalem.' "

Then everyone God had inspired prepared to go. They wanted to go up to Jerusalem and build the Lord's temple there. All their neighbors helped them. They gave them silver and gold objects. They gave them goods and livestock. And they gave them gifts of great value. All those things were added to the other offerings the people chose to give.

Ezra lists all the objects taken from God's temple that King Cyrus sent back with the people. He lists the number of people who returned from Babylon. He also lists the towns where their families came from.

The total number of the entire group that returned was 42,360. That didn't include their 7,337 male and female slaves. There were also 200 male and female singers. And there were 736 horses, 245 mules, 435 camels and 6,720 donkeys.

All the people arrived at the place in Jerusalem where the LORD's temple would be rebuilt. Then some of the leaders of the families brought offerings they chose to give. They would be used for rebuilding the house of God. It would stand in the same place it had been before. The people gave money for the work. It was based on how much they had. They gave 1,100 pounds of gold. They also gave three tons of silver. And they gave 100 sets of clothes for the priests. All of that was added to the temple treasure.

It was the second month of the second year after they had arrived at the house of God in Jerusalem. Zerubbabel, the son of Shealtiel, began the work. Joshua, the son of Jozadak, helped him. So did everyone else.

The builders laid the foundation of the LORD's temple. Then the priests came. They were wearing their special clothes. They brought their trumpets with them. The Levites who belonged to the family line of Asaph also came. They brought their cymbals with them. The priests and Levites took their places to praise the LORD. They did everything just as King David had required them to. They sang to the LORD. They praised him. They gave thanks to him. They said,

"The LORD is good.
His faithful love to Israel continues forever."

All the people gave a loud shout. They praised the LORD. They were glad because the foundation of the LORD's temple had been laid. But many of the older priests and Levites and family leaders wept out loud. They had seen the first temple. So when they saw the foundation of the second temple being laid, they wept. Others shouted with joy. No one could tell the difference between the shouts of joy and the sounds of weeping. That's because the people made so much noise. The sound was heard far away.

remember what you read

1. What is something you noticed for the first time?

_____

_____

_____

_____

2. What questions did you have?

_____

_____

_____

_____

3. Was there anything that bothered you?

_____

_____

_____

_____

4. What did you learn about loving God?

_____

_____

_____

_____

5. What did you learn about loving others?

_____

_____

_____

_____

EZRA, PART 2; NEHEMIAH, PART 1

The people who had returned from Babylon were building a temple to honor the LORD. The enemies of Judah and Benjamin heard about it. Then those enemies came to Zerubbabel. The family leaders of Israel were with him. The enemies said, "We want to help you build. We're just like you. We worship your God. We offer sacrifices to him. We've been doing that ever since the time of Esarhaddon. He was king of Assyria. He brought our people here."

Zerubbabel and Joshua answered them. So did the rest of the family leaders of Israel. They said, "You can't help us build a temple to honor our God. You aren't part of us. We'll build it ourselves. We'll do it to honor the LORD, the God of Israel. Cyrus, the king of Persia, commanded us to build it."

Then the nations around Judah tried to make its people lose hope. They wanted to make them afraid to go on building. So those nations paid some of the Jewish officials to work against the people of Judah. They wanted their plans to fail. They did it during the whole time Cyrus was king of Persia. They kept doing it until Darius became king.

The enemies of the Jews brought charges against the people of Judah and Jerusalem. It happened when Xerxes began to rule over Persia.

Later, these enemies wrote a letter to King Artaxerxes. This letter accused the Jewish people of rebelling in the past. King Artaxerxes searched records and found that Israel had been powerful. He thought it was dangerous to his empire for Jerusalem and the temple to be rebuilt. So he sent a letter telling the people to stop working.

And so the work on the house of God in Jerusalem came to a stop. No more work was done on it until the second year that Darius was king of Persia.

Haggai and Zechariah, the prophets, prophesied to the Jews in Judah and Jerusalem. They spoke to them in the name of the God of Israel. God had spoken to those prophets. Zerubbabel, the son of Shealtiel, began to work. So did Joshua, the son of Jozadak. They began to rebuild the house of God in Jerusalem. The prophets of God were right there with them. They were helping them.

At that time Tattenai was governor of the land west of the Euphrates River. He and Shethar-Bozenai and their friends went to the Jews. They asked them, "Who authorized you to rebuild this temple? Who told you that you could finish it?"

The governor sent a letter to King Darius. He asked if the king had said it was okay for the Jews to rebuild the temple. Darius searched the records. He found the order from King Cyrus to rebuild the temple. He also saw the order for the king to pay for the work. So Darius wrote a letter to Tattenai the governor to make the work on the temple continue.

The elders of the Jews continued to build the temple. They enjoyed great success because of the preaching of Haggai and Zechariah, the prophets. The people finished building the temple. That's what the God of Israel had commanded them to do. Cyrus and Darius had given orders allowing them to do it. Later, Artaxerxes supplied many things that were needed in the temple. Those three men were kings of Persia. So the temple was completed on the third day of the month of Adar. It was in the sixth year that Darius was king.

When the house of God was set apart, the people of Israel celebrated with joy. The priests and Levites joined them. So did the rest of those who had returned from the land of Babylon. When the house of God was set apart to him, the people sacrificed 100 bulls. They also sacrificed 200 rams and 400 male lambs. As a sin offering for the whole nation of Israel, the people sacrificed

12 male goats. One goat was sacrificed for each tribe in Israel. The priests were appointed to their groups. And the Levites were appointed to their groups. All of them served God at Jerusalem. They served him in keeping with what is written in the Book of Moses.

The people who had returned from the land of Babylon celebrated the Passover Feast. It was on the 14th day of the first month. The priests and Levites had made themselves pure and "clean." The Levites killed Passover lambs for the people who had returned from Babylon. They also did it for themselves and their relatives, the priests. So the Israelites who had returned ate the Passover lamb. They ate it together with all those who had separated themselves from the practices of their Gentile neighbors. Those practices were "unclean." The people worshiped the LORD. He is the God of Israel. For seven days they celebrated the Feast of Unleavened Bread with joy. That's because the LORD had filled them with joy. They were glad because he had changed the mind of the king of Persia. So the king had helped them with the work on the house of the God of Israel.

⚬⚬⚬

After all these things had happened, Ezra came up to Jerusalem from Babylon. It was during the rule of Artaxerxes. He was king of Persia. So Ezra came up from Babylon. The king had given Ezra everything he asked for. That's because the LORD his God helped him. It was in the seventh year that Artaxerxes was king.

Ezra had committed himself to study and obey the Law of the LORD. He also wanted to teach the LORD's rules and laws in Israel.

Ezra was a priest and teacher of the Law. He was an educated man. He knew the LORD's commands and rules for Israel very well.

King Artaxerxes gave a letter to Ezra. He gave Ezra many tons of gold, silver, wheat, wine, and olive oil to help the Jews. He wanted to be sure they were worshiping the God of Israel well. The king also told the governors not to collect taxes from anyone who worked in the temple. And he wanted Ezra to teach everyone to obey God's Law.

So here is what I, Ezra, say to you people of Israel. "Give praise to the LORD. He is the God of our people who lived long ago. He has put it in the king's heart to bring honor to the LORD's temple in Jerusalem. The king has honored the LORD in his letter. The LORD has been kind to me. He has caused the king and his advisers to be kind to me. In fact, all the king's powerful officials have been kind to me. The strong hand of the LORD my God helped me. That gave me new strength. So I gathered together leaders from Israel to go up to Jerusalem with me."

Ezra and the rest of the Jews from Babylon gave sacrifices, such as animals and foods, to God. Then some of the leaders in Jerusalem told Ezra they had married women from other nations. Ezra tore his clothes and cried. He was very sad and did not eat for days. God's Law told the people of Israel not to marry people from other nations because they would cause the Jews to worship other gods. This was the reason the people were taken to Babylon. So Ezra wanted to be very careful that everyone worshiped only the one true God. He told all the men to send away their wives who were from other nations. They were very sad, but they obeyed.

These are the words of Nehemiah. He was the son of Hakaliah.

I was in the fort of Susa. I was there in the 20th year that Artaxerxes was king. At that time Hanani came from Judah with some other men. He was one of my brothers. I asked him and the other men about the Jews who were left alive in Judah. They had returned from Babylon. I also asked him about Jerusalem.

He and the men with him said to me, "Some of the people who returned are still alive. They are back in the land of Judah. But they are having a hard time. They are ashamed. The wall of Jerusalem is broken down. Its gates have been burned with fire."

When I heard about these things, I sat down and wept. For several days I was very sad. I didn't eat any food. And I prayed to the God of heaven.

I was the king's wine taster. Wine was brought in for King Artaxerxes. I got the wine and gave it to him. I hadn't been sad in front of him before. But now I was. So the king asked me, "Why are you looking so sad? You aren't sick. You must be feeling very sad."

I was really afraid. But I said to the king, "May you live forever! Why shouldn't I look sad? The city where my people of long ago are buried has been destroyed. And fire has burned up its gates."

The king said to me, "What do you want?"

I prayed to the God of heaven. Then I answered the king, "Are you pleased with me, King Artaxerxes? If it pleases you, send me to Judah. Let me go to the city of Jerusalem. That's where my people are buried. I want to rebuild it."

The queen was sitting beside the king. He turned and asked me, "How long will your journey take? When will you get back?" It pleased the king to send me. So I chose a certain time.

I also said to him, "If it pleases you, may I take some letters with me? I want to give them to the governors of the land west of the Euphrates River. Then they'll help me travel safely through their territory until I arrive in Judah. May I also have a letter to Asaph? He takes care of the royal park. I want him to give me some logs so I can make beams out of them. I want to use them for the gates of the fort that is by the temple. Some of the logs will also be used in the city wall. And I'll need some for the house I'm going to live in." God was kind to me and helped me. So the king gave me what I asked for. Then I went to the governors of the land west of the Euphrates River. I gave them the king's letters. He had also sent army officers and horsemen along with me.

Sanballat and Tobiah heard about what was happening. Sanballat was a Horonite. Tobiah was an official from Ammon. They were very upset that someone had come to help the Israelites.

Nehemiah looked around Jerusalem. He saw how badly the wall was broken. He encouraged several different groups of people to work very hard. They set up gates around the city. These gates would allow people in and out after the wall was built.

Sanballat heard that we were rebuilding the wall. So he became very angry and upset. He made fun of the Jews. He spoke to his friends and the army of Samaria. He said, "What are those Jews trying to do? Can they make their city wall like new again? Will they offer sacrifices? Can they finish everything in a single day? The stones from their city wall and buildings are piled up like trash. And everything has been badly burned. Can they use those stones to rebuild everything again?"

I prayed to God. I said, "Our God, please listen to our prayer. Some people hate us. They're saying bad things about us. So let others say bad things about them. Let them be carried off like stolen goods. Let them be taken to another country as prisoners. Don't hide your eyes from their guilt. Don't forgive their sins. They have said bad things about the builders."

remember what you read

1. What is something you noticed for the first time?

_____

_____

_____

_____

2. What questions did you have?

_____

_____

_____

_____

3. Was there anything that bothered you?

_____

_____

_____

_____

4. What did you learn about loving God?

_____

_____

_____

_____

5. What did you learn about loving others?

_____

_____

_____

_____

So we rebuilt the wall. We repaired it until all of it was half as high as we wanted it to be. The people worked with all their heart.

But Sanballat and Tobiah heard that Jerusalem's walls continued to be repaired. The Arabs, the Ammonites and the people of Ashdod heard about it too. They heard that the gaps in the wall were being filled in. So they were very angry. All of them made evil plans to come and fight against Jerusalem. They wanted to stir up trouble against it. But we prayed to our God. We put guards on duty day and night to watch out for danger.

And our enemies said, "We will be right there among them. We'll kill them. We'll put an end to their work. We'll do it before they even know it or see us."

Then the Jews who lived near our enemies came to us. They told us ten times, "No matter where you are, they'll attack us."

So I stationed some people behind the lowest parts of the wall. That's where our enemies could easily attack us. I stationed the people family by family. They had their swords, spears and bows with them. I looked things over. Then I stood up and spoke to the nobles, the officials and the rest of the people. I said, "Don't be afraid of your enemies. Remember the Lord. He is great and powerful. So fight for your families. Fight for your sons and daughters. Fight for your wives and homes."

From that day on, half of my men did the work. The other half were given spears, shields, bows and armor. The officers stationed themselves behind all the people of Judah. The people continued to build the wall. The people who carried supplies did their work with one hand. They held a weapon in the other hand. Each of the builders wore his sword at his side as he worked. But the man who blew the trumpet stayed with me.

Then I spoke to the nobles, the officials and the rest of the people. I said, "This is a big job. It covers a lot of territory. We're separated too far from one another along the wall. When you hear the sound of the trumpet, join us at that location. Our God will fight for us!"

So we continued the work. Half of the men held spears. We worked from the first light of sunrise until the stars came out at night. At that time I also spoke to the people. I told them, "Have every man and his helper stay inside Jerusalem at night. Then they can guard us at night. And they can work during the day." My relatives and I didn't take off our clothes. My men and the guards didn't take theirs off either. Each man kept his weapon with him, even when he went to get water.

The enemies of the Jews tried many times to trick Nehemiah into meeting with them so they could kill him. But he refused and kept working.

You are my God. Remember what Tobiah and Sanballat have done. Also remember the prophet Noadiah. She and the rest of the prophets have been trying to scare me. So the city wall was completed on the 25th day of the month of Elul. It was finished in 52 days.

All our enemies heard about it. All the nations around us became afraid. They weren't sure of themselves anymore. They realized that our God had helped us finish the work.

෨෨෨

Ezra the priest brought the Law out to the whole community. It was the first day of the seventh month. The group was made up of men, women, and children old enough to understand what Ezra was going to read. He read the Law to them from sunrise until noon. He did it as he faced the open area in front of the Water Gate. He read it to the men, the women, and the children old enough to understand. And all the people paid careful attention as Ezra was reading the Book of the Law.

Ezra, the teacher of the Law, stood on a high wooden stage. It had been built for the occasion.

Ezra opened the book. All the people could see him. That's because he was standing above them. As he opened the book, the people stood up. Ezra praised the LORD. He is the great God. All the people lifted up their hands and said, "Amen! Amen!" Then they bowed down. They turned their faces toward the ground and worshiped the LORD.

The Levites taught the Law to the people. They remained standing while the Levites taught them. All these Levites read to the people parts of the Book of the Law of God. They made it clear to them. They told them what it meant. So the people understood what was being read.

Nehemiah was the governor. Ezra was a priest and the teacher of the Law. They spoke up. So did the Levites who were teaching the people. All these men said to the people, "This day is set apart to honor the LORD your God. So don't weep. Don't be sad." All the people had been weeping as they listened to the words of the Law.

Nehemiah said, "Go and enjoy some good food and sweet drinks. Send some of it to people who don't have any. This day is holy to our Lord. So don't be sad. The joy of the LORD makes you strong."

Then all the people went away to eat and drink. They shared their food with others. They celebrated with great joy. Now they understood the words they had heard. That's because everything had been explained to them.

All the family leaders gathered around Ezra, the teacher. So did the priests and Levites. All of them paid attention to the words of the Law. It was the second day of the month. The LORD had given the Law through Moses. He wanted the Israelites to obey it. It is written there that they were supposed to live in booths during the Feast of Booths. That feast was celebrated in the seventh month. They were also supposed to spread the message all through their towns and in Jerusalem. They were supposed to announce, "Go out into the central hill country. Bring back some branches from olive and wild olive trees. Also bring some from myrtle, palm and shade trees. Use the branches to make booths."

So the people went out and brought back some branches. They built themselves booths on their own roofs. They made them in their courtyards. They put them up in the courtyards of the house of God. They built them in the open area in front of the Water Gate. And they built them in the open area in front of the Gate of Ephraim. All the people who had returned from the land of Babylon made booths. They lived in them during the Feast of Booths. They hadn't celebrated the feast with so much joy for a long time. In fact, they had never celebrated it like that from the days of Joshua, the son of Nun, until that day. So their joy was very great.

Day after day, Ezra read parts of the Book of the Law of God to them. He read it out loud from the first day to the last. They celebrated the Feast of Booths for seven days. On the eighth day they gathered together. They followed the required rules for celebrating the feast.

It was the 24th day of the seventh month. The Israelites gathered together again. They didn't eat any food. They wore the rough clothing people wear when they're sad. They put dust on their heads. The Israelites separated themselves from everyone else. They stood and admitted they had sinned. They also admitted that their people before them had sinned. They stood where they were. They listened while the Levites read parts of the Book of the Law of the LORD their God. They listened for a fourth of the day. They spent another fourth of the day admitting their sins. They also worshiped the LORD their God. Some people were standing on the stairs of the Levites. With loud voices they called out to the LORD their God. Then some Levites spoke up. They said to the people, "Stand up. Praise the LORD your God. He lives for ever and ever!"

The people prayed a long prayer. They remembered how God had acted in powerful ways in their history. They also told God how they had disobeyed and asked for his forgiveness. They asked for God's help because their enemies were making it hard for them to live. Then the people made a covenant, a serious agreement with God and each other. They promised to not marry women from other nations. People from other nations would cause them to worship other "gods." They promised to not work on the Sabbath. And they promised to bring offerings to take care of the temple.

The wall of Jerusalem was set apart to God. For that occasion, the Levites were gathered together from where they lived. They were brought to Jerusalem to celebrate that happy occasion. They did it by singing and giving their thanks to him. They celebrated by playing music on cymbals, harps and lyres. The musicians were also brought together. The priests and Levites made themselves pure. Then they made the people, the gates and the wall pure and "clean."

I, Nehemiah, had the leaders of Judah go up on top of the wall. I also appointed two large choirs to sing and give thanks. I told one of them to walk south on top of the wall. That was toward the Dung Gate. Ezra led the group that was marching south. He was the teacher of the Law. At the Fountain Gate they continued straight up the steps of the City of David. The steps went up to the wall. Then the group passed above the place where David's palace had been. They continued on to the Water Gate on the east.

The second choir went north. I followed them on top of the wall. Half of the people went with me. They went past the Tower of the Ovens. They went to the Broad Wall. They marched over the Gate of Ephraim. They went over the Jeshanah Gate and the Fish Gate. They went past the Tower of Hananel and the Tower of the Hundred. They continued on to the Sheep Gate. At the Gate of the Guard they stopped.

Then the two choirs that sang and gave thanks took their places in God's house. So did I. So did half of the officials. And so did the priests. The choirs sang under the direction of Jezrahiah. On that day large numbers of sacrifices were offered. The people were glad because God had given them great joy. The women and children were also very happy. The joyful sound in Jerusalem could be heard far away.

I returned to the Persian King Artaxerxes, the king of Babylon. I went to him in the 32nd year of his rule. Some time later I asked him to let me return to Jerusalem.

When Nehemiah got back to Jerusalem, he found that the people were not taking care of the musicians and the temple. They were working on the Sabbath, and they were marrying women from other nations. They had promised not to do these things. So Nehemiah had to help the people keep their promises.

You are my God. Remember me because of what I've done. I've worked faithfully for your temple and its services. So please don't forget the good things I've done.

remember what you read

1. What is something you noticed for the first time?

_____

_____

_____

_____

2. What questions did you have?

_____

_____

_____

_____

3. Was there anything that bothered you?

_____

_____

_____

_____

4. What did you learn about loving God?

_____

_____

_____

_____

5. What did you learn about loving others?

_____

_____

_____

_____

introduction to Esther, parts 1-2

King Xerxes ruled over the kingdom of Persia after the kings before him conquered Babylon. This was after Babylon destroyed Jerusalem. His land stretched all the way from India to Egypt. The story of Esther begins when the king invited everyone who lived in his city to a giant party at his fantastic palace. The party lasted six months! Xerxes ordered Queen Vashti to stand in front of everyone so he could brag about how beautiful she was. But the queen refused. The king was so angry that he said she couldn't be queen anymore.

~

Later, the great anger of King Xerxes calmed down. At that time the king's personal attendants made a suggestion. They said, "King Xerxes, let a search be made for some beautiful young virgins for you. Appoint some officials in every territory in your kingdom. Have them bring all these beautiful young women into the fort of Susa. Then put Hegai in charge of them. He's the official who serves you. He's in charge of the women. Let beauty care be given to the new group of women. Then let the young woman who pleases you the most become queen in Vashti's place." The king liked that advice. So he followed it.

There was a Jew living in the fort of Susa. He was from the tribe of Benjamin. His name was Mordecai. Nebuchadnezzar had forced Mordecai to leave Jerusalem. He was among the prisoners who were carried off along with Jehoiachin. Jehoiachin had been king of Judah. Nebuchadnezzar was king of Babylon. Mordecai had a cousin named Hadassah. He had raised her because she didn't have a father or mother. Hadassah was also called Esther. She had a lovely figure and was very beautiful. Mordecai had adopted her as his own daughter.

After the king's order and law were announced, many young women were brought to the fort of Susa. Hegai was put in charge of them. Esther was also taken to the king's palace. She was put under the control of Hegai. Esther pleased him. He showed her how happy he was with her. Right away he provided her with her beauty care and special food. He appointed seven female attendants to help her.

Esther hadn't told anyone who her people were. She hadn't talked about her family. That's because Mordecai had told her not to. Mordecai tried to find out how Esther was getting along. He wanted to know what was happening to her. So he walked back and forth near the courtyard by the place where the virgins stayed. He did it every day.

Each young woman had to complete 12 months of beauty care. Everyone who saw Esther was pleased with her. She was taken to King Xerxes in the royal house. It was now the tenth month. That was the month of Tebeth. It was the seventh year of the rule of Xerxes.

The king liked Esther more than he liked any of the other women. She pleased him more than any of the other virgins. So he put a royal crown on her head. He made her queen in Vashti's place. Then the king gave a feast to honor Esther. All his nobles and officials were invited. He announced a holiday all through the territories he ruled over. He freely gave many gifts in keeping with his royal wealth.

Bigthana and Teresh were two of the king's officers. They guarded the door of the royal palace. They became angry with King Xerxes. So they decided to kill him. They made their evil plans while Mordecai was sitting at the palace gate. So Mordecai found out about it and told Queen Esther. Then she reported it to the king. She told him that Mordecai had uncovered the plans against him. Some people checked Esther's report. And they found out it was true. So the two officials were put to death. Then poles were stuck through them. They were set up where people could see them. All of that was written in the official records. It was written down while the king was watching.

After those events, King Xerxes honored Haman. He gave him a seat of honor. It was higher than the positions any of the other nobles had. All the royal officials at the palace gate got down on their knees. They gave honor to Haman. That's because the king had commanded them to do it. But Mordecai refused to get down on his knees. He wouldn't give Haman any honor at all.

The royal officials at the palace gate asked Mordecai a question. They said, "Why don't you obey the king's command?" Day after day they spoke to him. But he still refused to obey. So they told Haman about it. They wanted to see whether he would let Mordecai get away with what he was doing. Mordecai had told them he was a Jew.

Haman noticed that Mordecai wouldn't get down on his knees. So Haman was very angry. But he had found out who Mordecai's people were. So he didn't want to kill only Mordecai. He also looked for a way to destroy all Mordecai's people. They were Jews. He wanted to kill all of them everywhere in the kingdom of Xerxes.

Haman asked King Xerxes to make a law that all the Jews throughout his empire should be killed on a certain day. The king had messengers carry the message to all 127 parts of the empire.

Mordecai found out about everything that had been done. So he tore his clothes. He put on the rough clothing people wear when they're sad. He sat down in ashes. Then he went out into the city. He wept out loud. But he only went as far as the palace gate. That's because no one dressed in that rough clothing was allowed to go through it. All the Jews were very sad. They didn't eat anything. They wept and cried. Many of them put on the rough clothing people wear when they're sad. They were lying down in ashes.

They did all these things in every territory where the king's order and law had been sent.

Esther's male and female attendants came to her. They told her about Mordecai. So she became very troubled. She wanted him to take off his rough clothing. So she sent him other clothes to wear. But he wouldn't accept them. Then Esther sent for Hathak. He was one of the king's officials. He had been appointed to take care of her. She ordered him to find out what was troubling Mordecai. She wanted to know why he was so upset.

So Hathak went out to see Mordecai. He was in the open area in front of the palace gate. Mordecai told him everything that had happened to him. He told him about the exact amount of money Haman had promised to add to the royal treasures. He said Haman wanted it to be used to pay some men to destroy the Jews. Mordecai also gave Hathak a copy of the order. It commanded people to wipe out the Jews. The order had been sent from Susa. Mordecai told Hathak to show the order to Esther. He wanted Hathak to explain it to her. Mordecai told him to tell her to go and beg the king for mercy. Mordecai wanted her to make an appeal to the king for her people.

Hathak went back and reported to Esther what Mordecai had said. Then Esther directed him to give an answer to Mordecai. She told him to say, "There is a certain law that everyone knows about. It applies to any man or woman who approaches the king in the inner courtyard without being sent for. It says they must be put to death. But there is a way out. Suppose the king reaches out his gold scepter toward them. Then their lives will be spared. But 30 days have gone by since the king sent for me."

Esther's words were reported to Mordecai. Then he sent back an answer. He said, "You live in the king's palace. But don't think that just because you are there you will be the only Jew who will escape. What if you don't say anything at this time? Then help for the Jews will come from another place. But you and your family will die. Who knows? It's possible that you became queen for a time just like this."

Then Esther sent a reply to Mordecai. She said, "Go. Gather together all the Jews who are in Susa. And fast for my benefit.

Don't eat or drink anything for three days. Don't do it night or day. I and my attendants will fast just as you do. Then I'll go to the king. I'll do it even though it's against the law. And if I have to die, I'll die."

So Mordecai went away. He carried out all Esther's directions.

On the third day Esther put on her royal robes. She stood in the inner courtyard of the palace. It was in front of the king's hall. The king was sitting on his royal throne in the hall. He was facing the entrance. He saw Queen Esther standing in the courtyard. He was pleased with her. So he reached out toward her the gold scepter that was in his hand. Then Esther approached him. She touched the tip of the scepter.

The king asked, "What is it, Queen Esther? What do you want? I'll give it to you. I'll even give you up to half of my kingdom."

Esther replied, "King Xerxes, if it pleases you, come to a feast today. I've prepared it for you. Please have Haman come with you."

"Bring Haman at once," the king said to his servants. "Then we'll do what Esther asks."

So the king and Haman went to the feast Esther had prepared. As they were drinking wine, the king asked Esther the same question again. He said, "What do you want? I'll give it to you. What do you want me to do for you? I'll even give you up to half of my kingdom."

Esther replied, "Here is what I want. Here is my appeal to you. I hope you will be pleased to give me what I want. And I hope you will be pleased to listen to my appeal. If you are, I'd like you and Haman to come tomorrow to the feast I'll prepare for you. Then I'll answer your question."

That day Haman was happy. So he left the palace in a good mood. But then he saw Mordecai at the palace gate. He noticed that Mordecai didn't stand up when he walked by. In fact, Mordecai didn't have any respect for him at all. So he was very angry with him. But Haman was able to control himself. He went on home.

remember what you read

1. What is something you noticed for the first time?

_____

_____

_____

_____

2. What questions did you have?

_____

_____

_____

_____

3. Was there anything that bothered you?

_____

_____

_____

_____

4. What did you learn about loving God?

_____

_____

_____

_____

5. What did you learn about loving others?

_____

_____

_____

_____

Haman called together his friends and his wife Zeresh. He bragged to them about how rich he was. He talked about how many sons he had. He spoke about all the ways the king had honored him. He bragged about how the king had given him a high position. It was higher than the position of any of the other nobles and officials. "And that's not all," Haman added. "I'm the only person Queen Esther invited to come with the king to the feast she gave. Now she has invited me along with the king tomorrow. But even all of that doesn't satisfy me. I won't be satisfied as long as I see that Jew Mordecai sitting at the palace gate."

Haman's wife Zeresh and all his friends said to him, "Get a pole. In the morning, ask the king to have Mordecai put to death. Have the pole stuck through his body. Set it up at a place where it will be 75 feet above the ground. Everyone will be able to see it there. Then go to the feast with the king. Have a good time." Haman was delighted with that suggestion. So he got the pole ready.

That night the king couldn't sleep. So he ordered the official records of his rule to be brought in. He ordered someone to read them to him. What Mordecai had done was written there. He had uncovered the plans of Bigthana and Teresh. They were two of the king's officers who guarded the door of the royal palace. They had decided to kill King Xerxes.

"What great honor has Mordecai received for doing that?" the king asked.

"Nothing has been done for him," his attendants answered.

The king asked, "Who is in the courtyard?" Haman had just entered the outer courtyard of the palace. He had come to speak to the king about putting Mordecai to death. He wanted to talk about putting Mordecai's body on the pole he had prepared for him.

The king's attendants said to him, "Haman is standing in the courtyard."

"Bring him in," the king ordered.

Haman entered. Then the king asked him, "What should be done for the man I want to honor?"

Haman said to himself, "Is there anyone the king would rather honor than me?" So he answered the king. He said, "Here is what you should do for the man you want to honor. Have your servants get a royal robe you have worn. Have them bring a horse you have ridden on. Have a royal mark placed on its head. Then give the robe and horse to one of your most noble princes. Let the robe be put on the man you want to honor. Let him be led on the horse through the city streets. Let people announce in front of him, 'This is what is done for the man the king wants to honor!'"

"Go right away," the king commanded Haman. "Get the robe. Bring the horse. Do exactly what you have suggested. Do it for Mordecai the Jew. He's sitting out there at the palace gate. Make sure you do everything you have suggested."

So Haman got the robe and the horse. He put the robe on Mordecai. And he led him on horseback through the city streets. He walked along in front of him and announced, "This is what is done for the man the king wants to honor!"

After that, Mordecai returned to the palace gate. But Haman rushed home. He covered his head because he was very sad. He told his wife Zeresh everything that had happened to him. He also told all his friends.

His advisers and his wife Zeresh spoke to him. They said, "Your fall from power started with Mordecai. He's a Jew. So now you can't stand up against him. You are going to be destroyed!" They were still talking with him when the king's officials arrived. They hurried Haman away to the feast Esther had prepared.

So the king and Haman went to Queen Esther's feast. They were drinking wine on the second day. The king again asked, "What do you want, Queen Esther? I'll give it to you. What do you want me to do for you? I'll even give you up to half of my kingdom."

Then Queen Esther answered, "Your Majesty, I hope you will be pleased to let me live. That's what I want. Please spare my people. That's my appeal to you. My people and I have been sold to be destroyed. We've been sold to be killed and wiped out. Suppose we had only been sold as male and female slaves. Then I wouldn't have said anything. That kind of suffering wouldn't be a good enough reason to bother you."

King Xerxes asked Queen Esther, "Who is the man who has dared to do such a thing? And where is he?"

Esther said, "The man hates us! He's our enemy! He's this evil Haman!"

Then Haman was terrified in front of the king and queen. The king got up. He was very angry. He left his wine and went out into the palace garden. But Haman realized that the king had already decided what he was going to do to him. So he stayed behind to beg Queen Esther for his life.

The king returned from the palace garden to the dinner hall. Just then he saw Haman falling on the couch where Esther was lying.

The king shouted, "Will he even treat the queen like this? Will he harm her while she's right here with me in the palace?"

As soon as the king finished speaking, his men covered Haman's face. Then Harbona said, "There's a pole standing near Haman's house. He has prepared it for Mordecai. Mordecai is the one who spoke up to help you. Haman had planned to have him put to death. He was going to have the pole stuck through his body. Then he was going to set it up at a place where it would be 75 feet above the ground." Harbona was one of the officials who attended the king.

The king said to his men, "Put Haman to death! Stick the pole through his body! Set it up where everyone can see it!" So they did. And they used the pole Haman had prepared for Mordecai. Then the king's anger calmed down.

That same day King Xerxes gave Queen Esther everything Haman had owned. Haman had been the enemy of the Jews. Esther had told the king that Mordecai was her cousin. So Mordecai came to see the king. The king took his ring off. It had his royal mark on it. He had taken it back from Haman. Now he gave it to Mordecai. And Esther put Mordecai in charge of everything Haman had owned.

King Xerxes gave Queen Esther and Mordecai the power to send out a new law to the whole empire. This allowed all the Jews to protect themselves. They could take whatever belonged to whoever attacked them.

Mordecai left the king and went on his way. Mordecai was wearing royal clothes when he went. They were blue and white. He was also wearing a large gold crown. And he was wearing a purple coat. It was made out of fine linen. The city of Susa celebrated with great joy. The Jews were filled with joy and happiness. They were very glad because now they were being honored. They celebrated and enjoyed good food. That was true everywhere the king's order came. Many people from other nations announced that they had become Jews. That's because they were so afraid of the Jews.

⟳⟳⟳

The king's order had to be carried out on the 13th day of the 12th month. That was the month of Adar. On that day the enemies of the Jews had hoped to win the battle over them. But now everything had changed. The Jews had gained the advantage over those who hated them. The Jews gathered together in their cities. They gathered in all the territories King Xerxes ruled over. They came together to attack those who were trying to destroy them. No one could stand up against them. The people from all the other nations were afraid of them. All the nobles in the territories helped the Jews. So did the royal officials, the governors and the king's officers. That's because they were so afraid of Mordecai. He was well known in the palace. His fame spread all through the territories. So he became more and more important.

The Jews struck down with swords all their enemies. They killed them and destroyed them. They did what they pleased to those who hated them. The Jews killed 500 men. They destroyed them in the fort of Susa. They also killed the ten sons of Haman. Haman had been the enemy of the Jews. They didn't take anything that belonged to their enemies.

The Jews in Susa also came together on the 14th day of the month of Adar. They put 300 men to death in Susa. But they didn't take anything that belonged to those men.

During that time, the rest of the Jews also gathered together. They lived in the king's territories. They came together to fight for their lives. They didn't want their enemies to bother them anymore. They wanted to get some peace and rest. So they killed 75,000 of their enemies. But they didn't take anything that belonged to them. It happened on the 13th of Adar. On the 14th day they rested. They made it a day to celebrate with great joy. And they enjoyed good food.

But the Jews in Susa had gathered together on the 13th and 14th. Then on the 15th they rested. They made it a day to celebrate with great joy. And they enjoyed good food.

That's why Jews who live out in the villages celebrate on the 14th of Adar. They celebrate that day with great joy. And they enjoy good food. They also give presents to each other on that day.

Mordecai wrote down everything that happened. He sent letters to all the Jews in all the territories of Persia. He told them to celebrate a feast on the 14th and 15th days of Adar every year. It would be called Purim after the pur, or lot, that the evil Haman used to decide the day of destruction.

⚬〰〰〰⚬

King Xerxes required people all through his kingdom to bring gifts. King Xerxes required gifts from its farthest shores. All the king's powerful and mighty acts are written down. That includes the whole story of how important Mordecai was. The king had given him a position of great honor. All these things are written in the official records of the kings of Media and Persia. The position of Mordecai the Jew was second only to the position of King Xerxes. Mordecai was the most important Jew. All the other Jews had the highest respect for him. That's because he worked for the good of his people. And he spoke up for the benefit of all the Jews.

remember what you read

1. What is something you noticed for the first time?

_____

_____

_____

_____

2. What questions did you have?

_____

_____

_____

_____

3. Was there anything that bothered you?

_____

_____

_____

_____

4. What did you learn about loving God?

_____

_____

_____

_____

5. What did you learn about loving others?

_____

_____

_____

_____

introduction to Daniel, part 1

The book of Daniel tells about the life of a young man from Jerusalem. It explains how he was taken from his home to serve the king of Babylon. Later, he served the king of Persia. The first half of the book tells how he wisely explained the kings' dreams and visions to them.

◦◦◦

Daniel and his friends were taken to Babylon when King Nebuchadnezzar conquered Jerusalem. His friends were renamed Shadrach, Meshach and Abednego. The king wanted all the young men he captured to be trained. He wanted them to help him run his empire. As part of the training, they were supposed to eat the food the king ate. But Daniel asked to eat just vegetables and drink water, since the king's food was "unclean." The person in charge was scared they would become weak and look bad, but Daniel asked for a ten-day test.

After the ten days Daniel and his friends looked healthy and well fed. In fact, they looked better than any of the young men who ate the king's food. So the guard didn't require them to eat the king's special food. He didn't require them to drink the king's wine either. He gave them vegetables instead.

God gave knowledge and understanding to these four young men. So they understood all kinds of writings and subjects. And Daniel could understand all kinds of visions and dreams. The king talked with them. He didn't find anyone equal to Daniel, Hananiah, Mishael and Azariah. The king always found their answers to be the best. Other men in his kingdom claimed to get knowledge by using magic. But the answers of Daniel and his friends were ten times better than theirs.

In the second year of Nebuchadnezzar's rule, he had a dream. His mind was troubled. He couldn't sleep. So the king sent for those who claimed to get knowledge by using magic. He also sent for those who practiced evil magic and those who studied the heavens. He wanted them to tell him what he had dreamed. They came in and stood in front of the king. He said to them, "I had a dream. It troubles me. So I want to know what it means."

The magicians asked the king to tell them the dream. But he would not. He said if they really got knowledge through magic, they should be able to tell him the dream. The king got so angry, he told his guards to kill all the magicians. When Daniel heard this, he and his friends worshiped God and asked him to help Daniel understand the dream.

Then Daniel went to Arioch. The king had appointed him to put the wise men of Babylon to death. Daniel said to him, "Don't kill the wise men of Babylon. Take me to the king. I'll tell him what his dream means."

Nebuchadnezzar spoke to Daniel, who was also called Belteshazzar. The king asked him, "Are you able to tell me what I saw in my dream? And can you tell me what it means?"

Daniel replied, "You have asked us to explain a mystery to you. But no wise man can do that. And those who try to figure things out by using magic can't do it either. But there is a God in heaven who can explain mysteries. King Nebuchadnezzar, he has shown you what is going to happen. Here is what you dreamed while lying in bed. And here are the visions that passed through your mind.

"King Nebuchadnezzar, you looked up and saw a large statue standing in front of you. It was huge. It shone brightly. And it terrified you. The head of the statue was made out of pure gold. Its chest and arms were made out of silver. Its stomach and thighs were made out of bronze. Its legs were made out of iron. And its feet were partly iron and partly baked clay. While you were watching, a rock was cut out. But human hands didn't do it. It struck the statue on its feet of iron and clay. It smashed them. Then the iron and clay were broken to pieces. So were the bronze, silver and gold. All of them were broken to pieces. They became like straw on a threshing floor at harvest time. The wind blew them away without leaving a trace. But the rock that struck the statue became a huge mountain. It filled the whole earth.

Daniel explained the dream. The head of gold was Nebuchadnezzar. Later, other weaker kingdoms would come.

"In the time of those kings, the God of heaven will set up a kingdom. It will never be destroyed. And no other nation will ever take it over. It will crush all those other kingdoms. It will bring them to an end. But it will last forever. That's what the vision of the rock cut out of a mountain means. Human hands didn't cut out the rock. It broke the statue to pieces. It smashed the iron, bronze, clay, silver and gold.

King Nebuchadnezzar gave Daniel and his friends important positions in Babylon.

King Nebuchadnezzar made a gold statue. It was 90 feet tall and 9 feet wide. He set it up on the plain of Dura near the city of Babylon.

The king ordered all his officials to bow down to the statue when they heard music play. If someone did not bow, they would be thrown into a flaming furnace. But Daniel's friends refused to bow to anyone other than the God of Israel. Nebuchadnezzar was very angry. But he offered them one more chance.

Shadrach, Meshach and Abednego replied to him. They said, "King Nebuchadnezzar, we don't need to talk about this anymore. We might be thrown into the blazing furnace. But the God we serve is able to bring us out of it alive. He will save us from your power. But we want you to know this, Your Majesty. Even if we knew that our God wouldn't save us, we still wouldn't serve your gods. We wouldn't worship the gold statue you set up."

Then Nebuchadnezzar was very angry with Shadrach, Meshach and Abednego. The look on his face changed. And he ordered that the furnace be heated seven times hotter than usual. He also gave some of the strongest soldiers in his army a command. He ordered them to tie up Shadrach, Meshach and Abednego. Then he told his men to throw them into the blazing furnace. So they were tied up. Then they were thrown into the furnace. They were wearing their robes, pants, turbans and other clothes. The king's command was carried out quickly. The furnace was so hot that its flames killed the soldiers who threw Shadrach, Meshach and Abednego into it. So the three men were firmly tied up. And they fell into the blazing furnace.

Then King Nebuchadnezzar leaped to his feet. He was so amazed he asked his advisers, "Didn't we tie up three men? Didn't we throw three men into the fire?"

They replied, "Yes, we did, Your Majesty."

The king said, "Look! I see four men walking around in the fire. They aren't tied up. And the fire hasn't even harmed them. The fourth man looks like a son of the gods."

Then the king approached the opening of the blazing furnace. He shouted, "Shadrach, Meshach and Abednego, come out! You who serve the Most High God, come here!"

So they came out of the fire. The royal rulers, high officials, governors and advisers crowded around them. They saw that the fire hadn't harmed their bodies. Not one hair on their heads was burned. Their robes weren't burned either. And they didn't even smell like smoke.

King Nebuchadnezzar honored the three young men and their God. Later, he had another dream. It terrified him, but he didn't know what it meant. Daniel was able to tell him what it meant. The very tall tree that he saw would be cut down. The tree was the king. He would become like an animal and live in the fields. He would eat grass. But after some time, God would restore his mind and give his kingdom back to him. One day, Nebuchadnezzar was walking on his palace roof. He was proud of everything he built, even though he hurt people to do it. *So God punished him by making him like an animal. After he was made better, he sent a letter to all the nations. He wanted them to know how the Most High God took care of him.*

King Belshazzar gave a huge banquet. He invited a thousand of his nobles to it. He drank wine with them. While Belshazzar was drinking his wine, he gave orders to his servants. He commanded them to bring in some gold and silver cups. They were the cups his father Nebuchadnezzar had taken from the temple in Jerusalem. Belshazzar had them brought in so everyone could drink from them. As they drank the wine, they praised their gods. The statues of those gods were made out of gold, silver, bronze, iron, wood or stone.

Suddenly the fingers of a human hand appeared. They wrote something on the plaster of the palace wall. The king watched the hand as it wrote. His face turned pale. He was so afraid that his legs became weak. And his knees were knocking together.

The king asked for someone to explain what the writing meant. He promised gifts and a powerful position. The queen told him about Daniel, who had served his father, Nebuchadnezzar. The king called for Daniel.

Then Daniel answered the king. He said, "You can keep your gifts for yourself. You can give your rewards to someone else. But I will read the writing for you. I'll tell you what it means."

Daniel explained that the king knew how his father's pride made him have to live like an animal. He said the pride that led the king to drink from cups from God's temple and praise his own gods was offensive to God. So God would remove him as king.

"Here is what was written.

MENE, MENE, TEKEL, PARSIN

"And here is what these words mean.

The word Mene means that God has limited the time of your rule. He has brought it to an end.

The word Tekel means that you have been weighed on scales. And you haven't measured up to God's standard.

The word Peres means that your authority over your kingdom will be taken away from you. It will be given to the Medes and Persians."

That very night Belshazzar, the king of Babylon, was killed. His kingdom was given to Darius the Mede. Darius was 62 years old.

It pleased Darius to appoint 120 royal rulers over his entire kingdom. He placed three leaders over them. One of the leaders was Daniel. The royal rulers were made accountable to the three leaders. Daniel did a better job than the other two leaders or any of the royal rulers. He was an unusually good and able man. So the king planned to put him in charge of the whole kingdom. But the other two leaders and the royal rulers heard about it. They tried to find something wrong with the way he ran the government. But they weren't able to. They couldn't find any fault with his work. He could always be trusted. He never did anything wrong. And he always did what he was supposed to. Finally these men said, "We want to bring charges against this man Daniel. But it's almost impossible for us to come up with a reason to do it. If we find a reason, it will have to be in connection with the law of his God."

All the leaders went to the king and suggested that he make a law. No one would be allowed to pray to anyone except King Darius for the next 30 days. The law could not be changed for any reason. Daniel heard about the law. He always prayed to the God of Israel while on his knees by his window. So he prayed to God anyway. The leaders told the king that Daniel broke the law.

When the king heard this, he was very upset. He didn't want Daniel to be harmed in any way. Until sunset, he did everything he could to save him.

Then the men went as a group to King Darius. They said to him,

"Your Majesty, remember that no order or command you give can be changed. That's what the law of the Medes and Persians requires."

So the king gave the order. Daniel was brought out and thrown into the lions' den. The king said to him, "You always serve your God faithfully. So may he save you!"

A stone was brought and placed over the opening of the den. The king sealed it with his own special ring. Then nothing could be done to help Daniel. The king returned to his palace. He didn't eat anything that night. And he couldn't sleep.

As soon as the sun began to rise, the king got up. He hurried to the lions' den. When he got near it, he called out to Daniel. His voice was filled with great concern. He said, "Daniel! You serve the living God. You always serve him faithfully. So has he been able to save you from the lions?"

Daniel answered, "Your Majesty, may you live forever! My God sent his angel. And his angel shut the mouths of the lions. They haven't hurt me at all. That's because I haven't done anything wrong in God's sight. I've never done anything wrong to you either, Your Majesty."

The king was filled with joy. He ordered his servants to lift Daniel out of the den. So they did. They didn't see any wounds on him. That's because he had trusted in his God.

Then the king gave another order. The men who had said bad things about Daniel were brought in. They were thrown into the lions' den. So were their wives and children. Before they hit the bottom of the den, the lions attacked them. And the lions crushed all their bones.

Then King Darius wrote to people of all nations, no matter what language they spoke. He said,

"May you have great success!

"I order people in every part of my kingdom to respect and honor Daniel's God.

"He is the living God.
   He will live forever.

His kingdom will not be destroyed.
    His rule will never end.
He sets people free and saves them.
    He does miraculous signs and wonders.
    He does them in the heavens and on the earth.
He has saved Daniel
    from the power of the lions."

So Daniel had success while Darius was king. Things went well with Daniel during the rule of Cyrus, the Persian.

remember what you read

1. What is something you noticed for the first time?

_____

_____

_____

_____

2. What questions did you have?

_____

_____

_____

_____

3. Was there anything that bothered you?

_____

_____

_____

_____

4. What did you learn about loving God?

_____

_____

_____

_____

5. What did you learn about loving others?

_____

_____

_____

_____

DANIEL, PART 2

introduction to Daniel, part 2

Daniel saw dreams and visions. Angels came to explain what he saw. Each vision showed Daniel what would happen in the future. Most of the visions pointed to a king of Syria named Antiochus IV. He did terrible things in the temple in Jerusalem in 168 BC. But there are other things the angels told Daniel that might not have happened yet. Whatever happens, we remember the vision of the kingdom of God that fills the whole earth and never ends.

It was the first year that Belshazzar was king of Babylon. Daniel had a dream. He was lying in bed. In his dream, visions passed through his mind. He wrote down what he saw.

Daniel saw four strange animals coming out of the sea. The first was like a lion with eagle's wings. The second was like a bear. The third was like a leopard with four wings and four heads. The fourth was terrifying and had many horns.

"In my vision I saw one who looked like a son of man. He was coming with the clouds of heaven. He approached the Eternal God. He was led right up to him. And he was given authority, glory and a kingdom. People of all nations, no matter what language they spoke, worshiped him. His authority will last forever. It will not pass away. His kingdom will never be destroyed.

*An angel explained the dream. It was very similar to the one
Nebuchadnezzar saw. These animals were four kingdoms. And after
the fourth kingdom, God set up a kingdom that will last forever.*

*Daniel had another vision. He saw a very strong ram. It trampled
everything in its path. No animal could resist it. Then a goat came
from the west and knocked the ram down. The goat stomped on the
ram. The angel Gabriel explained the vision. The ram was Persia. The
goat would be Greece. The goat's big horn broke off and four other
horns took its place. The angel explained that Greece would break into
four parts. (This all happened after Alexander the Great died.)*

It was the first year that Darius was king of Babylon. He was
from Media and was the son of Xerxes. In that year I learned from
the Scriptures that Jerusalem would remain destroyed for 70
years. That was what the LORD had told Jeremiah the prophet. So
I prayed to the Lord God. I begged him. I made many appeals to
him. I didn't eat anything. I put on the rough clothing people wear
when they're sad. And I sat down in ashes.

I prayed to the LORD my God. I admitted that we had sinned. I
said,

"Lord, you are a great and wonderful God. You keep the covenant you made with all those who love you and obey your
commandments. You show them your love. We have sinned
and done what is wrong. We have been evil. We have refused
to obey you. We have turned away from your commands and
laws. We haven't listened to your servants the prophets. They
spoke in your name to our kings, our princes and our people
of long ago. They also brought your message to all our people
in the land.

"Lord, you always do what is right. But we are covered with
shame today. We are the people of Judah and Jerusalem. All of
us are Israelites, no matter where we live. We are now living in
many countries. You scattered us among the nations because
we weren't faithful to you. We have sinned against you. You are
the Lord our God. You show us your tender love. You forgive
us. But we have turned against you. You are the LORD our God.

"Curses and warnings are written down in the Law of Moses. He was your servant. Those curses have been poured out on us. That's because we have sinned against you.

"Lord our God, you used your mighty hand to bring your people out of Egypt. You made a name for yourself. It is still great to this day. But we have sinned. We've done what is wrong. Lord, you saved your people before. So turn your great anger away from Jerusalem again. After all, it is your city. It's your holy mountain. You have made those who live around us think little of Jerusalem and your people. That's because we have sinned. Our people before us did evil things too.

"Our God, hear my prayers. Pay attention to the appeals I make to you. Lord, have mercy on your temple that has been destroyed. Do it for your own honor. Our God, please listen to us. The city that belongs to you has been destroyed. Open your eyes and see it. We aren't asking you to answer our prayers because we are godly. Instead, we're asking you to do it because you love us so much. Lord, please listen! Lord, please forgive us! Lord, hear our prayers! Take action for your own honor. Our God, please don't wait. Your city and your people belong to you."

Gabriel explained to Daniel that the 70 years were actually 70 "weeks" of years. This was split into seven "weeks" and 62 "weeks" and one final "week." The first 49 years would begin with Cyrus's order to rebuild the temple. Then after that would be 434 years until the Anointed King would be killed. (Christians understand this to be Jesus.) The last seven years point to the "end." People today have different ideas about what the end looks like.

It was the third year that Cyrus, the king of Persia, ruled over Babylon. At that time I was living in Babylon. There the people called me Belteshazzar. A message from God came to me. It was true. It was about a great war. I had a vision that showed me what it meant.

At that time I was very sad for three weeks. I didn't eat any rich food. No meat or wine touched my lips. I didn't use any lotions at all until the three weeks were over.

I was standing on the bank of the great Tigris River. It was the 24th day of the first month. I looked up and saw a man dressed in linen clothes. He had a belt around his waist. It was made out of fine gold from Uphaz. His body gleamed like topaz. His face shone like lightning. His eyes were like flaming torches. His arms and legs were as bright as polished bronze. And his voice was like the sound of a large crowd.

I was the only one who saw the vision. The people who were there with me didn't see it. But they were so terrified that they ran and hid. So I was left alone as I was watching this great vision. I felt very weak. My face turned as pale as death. And I was helpless. Then I heard the man speak. As I listened to him, I fell sound asleep. My face was toward the ground.

An angel touched Daniel. He encouraged him and made him strong. Then he explained what was going to happen in the future. He told about the king of Greece (Alexander the Great). The king's sons would not be king after him. Four other people would split his kingdom. The vision of the future talked about several kings of Egypt and Syria. Finally a king of Syria (Antiochus IV) would set an idol in God's temple. He would kill the people of Israel if they kept the law of God. So Israel would suffer, but they would become pure.

(The rest of Daniel can be hard to understand. Some of it probably happened around the time of Jesus. Some of it might be coming in the future.)

"A certain king will do as he pleases. He will honor himself. He will put himself above every god. He will say things against the greatest God of all. Those things have never been heard before. He will have success until God is not angry anymore. What God has decided to do must take place. The king will not show any respect for the gods his people have always worshiped. There is a god desired by women. He will not respect that god either. He will not have respect for any god. Instead, he will put himself above all of them. In place of them, he will worship a god of war. He will honor a god his people have not known before. He will give gold and silver to that god. He will bring jewels and expensive gifts to it. He will attack the strongest forts. A new god will help him do it. He will greatly honor those who recognize him as their leader. He will make them rulers over many people. And he will give them land as a reward.

"A king in the south will go to war against him. It will happen at the time of the end. The king who will honor himself will rush out against him. He will come with chariots and horsemen. He will attack with a lot of ships. He will lead his army into many countries. He will sweep through them like a flood. He will also march into the beautiful land of Israel. Many countries will fall. But Edom, Moab and the leaders of Ammon will be saved from his mighty hand. His power will reach out into many countries. Even Egypt will not escape. He will gain control of all Egypt's riches. He will take their gold and silver treasures. The people of Libya and Cush will be under his control. But reports from the east and the north will terrify him. He will march out with great anger to destroy many people and wipe them out. He will set up his royal tents. He will put them between the Mediterranean Sea and the beautiful holy mountain of Zion. But his end will come. And no one will help him.

"At that time Michael will appear. He is the great prince of the angels. He guards your people. There will be a time of terrible suffering. Things will be worse than at any time since nations began. But at that time of suffering your people will be saved. Their names are written in the book of life. Many people who lie dead in their graves will wake up. Some will rise up to life that will never end. Others will rise up to shame that will never end. Those who are wise will shine like the brightness of the sky. Those who lead many others to do what is right will be like the stars for ever and ever. But I want you to roll up this scroll, Daniel. Seal it until the time of the end. Many people will go here and there to increase their knowledge."

Then I looked up and saw two other angels. One was on this side of the Tigris River. And one was on the other side. The man who was dressed in linen was above the waters of the river. One of the angels spoke to him. He asked, "How long will it be before these amazing things come true?"

The man raised both hands toward heaven. I heard him make a promise in the name of the God who lives forever. He answered me, "Three and a half years. Then the power of the holy people will finally be broken. And all these things will come true."

I heard what he said. But I didn't understand it. So I asked, "My master, what will come of all this?"

He answered, "Go on your way, Daniel. The scroll is rolled up. It is sealed until the time of the end. Many people will be made pure in the fire. They will be made spotless. But sinful people will continue to be evil. Not one sinful person will understand. But those who are wise will.

"The daily sacrifices will be stopped. And the hated thing that destroys will be set up. After that, there will be 1,290 days. Blessed are those who wait for the 1,335 days and reach the end of them.

"Daniel, go on your way until the end. Your body will rest in the grave. Then at the end of the days you will rise from the dead. And you will receive what God has appointed for you."

remember what you read

1. What is something you noticed for the first time?

_____

_____

_____

_____

2. What questions did you have?

_____

_____

_____

_____

3. Was there anything that bothered you?

_____

_____

_____

_____

4. What did you learn about loving God?

_____

_____

_____

_____

5. What did you learn about loving others?

_____

_____

_____

_____

A Word About
The New International Reader's Version

Have You Ever Heard of the New International Version?

We call it the NIV. Many people read the NIV. In fact, more people read the NIV than any other English Bible. They like it because it's easy to read and understand.

And now we are happy to give you another Bible that's easy to read and understand. It's the New International Reader's Version. We call it the NIrV.

Who Will Enjoy Reading the New International Reader's Version?

People who are just starting to read will understand and enjoy the NIrV. Children will be able to read it and understand it. So will older people who are learning how to read. People who are reading the Bible for the first time will be able to enjoy reading the NIrV. So will people who have a hard time understanding what they read. And so will people who use English as their second language. We hope this Bible will be just right for you.

How Is the NIrV Different From the NIV?

The NIrV is based on the NIV. The NIV Committee on Bible Translation (CBT) didn't produce the NIrV. But a few of us who worked on the NIrV are members of CBT. We worked hard to make the NIrV possible. We used the words of the NIV when we could. When the words of the NIV were too long, we used shorter words. We tried to use words that are easy to understand. We also made the sentences of the NIV much shorter.

Why did we do all these things? Because we wanted to make the NIrV very easy to read and understand.

What Other Helps Does the NIrV Have?

We decided to give you a lot of other help too. For example, sometimes a verse is quoted from another place in the Bible. When it is, we tell you the Bible book, chapter and verse it comes from. We put that information right after the verse that quotes from another place.

We separated each chapter into shorter sections. We gave a title to almost every chapter. Sometimes we even gave a title to a section. We did these things to help you understand what the chapter or section is all about.

Another example of a helpful change has to do with the word "Selah" in the Psalms. What this Hebrew word means is still not clear. So, for now, this word is not helpful for readers. The NIV has moved the word to the bottom of the page. We have followed the NIV and removed this Hebrew word from the NIrV. Perhaps one day we will learn what this word means. But until then, the Psalms are easier to read and understand without it.

Sometimes the writers of the Bible used more than one name for the same person or place. For example, in the New Testament the Sea of Galilee is also called the Sea of Gennesaret. Sometimes it is also called the Sea of Tiberias. But in the NIrV we decided to call it the Sea of Galilee everywhere it appears. We called it that because that is its most familiar name.

We also wanted to help you learn the names of people and places in the Bible. So sometimes we provided names even in verses where those names don't actually appear. For example, sometimes the Bible says "the River" where it means "the Euphrates River." In those places, we used the full name "the Euphrates River." Sometimes the word "Pharaoh" in the Bible means "Pharaoh Hophra." In those places, we used his full name "Pharaoh Hophra." We did all these things in order to make the NIrV as clear as possible.

Does the NIrV Say What the First Writers of the Bible Said?

We wanted the NIrV to say just what the first writers of the Bible said. So we kept checking the Greek New Testament as we did our work. That's because the New Testament's first writers used Greek. We also kept checking the Hebrew Old Testament as we did our work. That's because the Old Testament's first writers used Hebrew.

We used the best copies of the Greek New Testament. We also used the best copies of the Hebrew Old Testament. Older English Bibles couldn't use those copies because they had not yet been found. The oldest copies are best because they are closer in time to the ones the first Bible writers wrote. That's why we kept checking the older copies instead of the newer ones.

Some newer copies of the Greek New Testament added several verses that the older ones don't have. Sometimes it's several verses in a row. This occurs at Mark 16:9–20 and John 7:53—8:11. We have included these verses in the NIrV. Sometimes the newer copies added only a single verse. An example is Mark 9:44. That verse is not in the oldest Greek New Testaments. So we put the verse number 43/44 right before Mark 9:43. You can look on the list below for Mark 9:44 and locate the verse that was added.

Verses That Were Not Found in Oldest Greek New Testaments

Matthew 17:21	But that kind does not go out except by prayer and fasting.
Matthew 18:11	The Son of Man came to save what was lost.
Matthew 23:14	How terrible for you, teachers of the law and Pharisees! You pretenders! You take over the houses of widows. You say long prayers to show off. So God will punish you much more.
Mark 7:16	Everyone who has ears to hear should listen.
Mark 9:44	In hell, / " 'the worms don't die, / and the fire doesn't go out.'
Mark 9:46	In hell, / " 'the worms don't die, / and the fire doesn't go out.'
Mark 11:26	But if you do not forgive, your Father who is in heaven will not forgive your sins either.
Mark 15:28	Scripture came true. It says, "And he was counted among those who disobey the law."
Luke 17:36	Two men will be in the field. One will be taken and the other left.
Luke 23:17	It was Pilate's duty to let one prisoner go free for them at the Feast.
John 5:4	From time to time an angel of the Lord would come down. The angel would stir up the waters. The first disabled person to go into the pool after it was stirred would be healed.
Acts 8:37	Philip said, "If you believe with all your heart, you can." The official answered, "I believe that Jesus Christ is the Son of God."
Acts 15:34	But Silas decided to remain there.
Acts 24:7	But Lysias, the commander, came. By using a lot of force, he took Paul from our hands.
Acts 28:29	After he said that, the Jews left. They were arguing strongly among themselves.
Romans 16:24	May the grace of our Lord Jesus Christ be with all of you. Amen.

What Is Our Prayer for You?

The Lord has blessed the New International Version in a wonderful way. He has used it to help millions of Bible readers. Many people have put their faith in Jesus after reading it. Many others have become stronger believers because they have read it.

We hope and pray that the New International Reader's Version will help you in the same way. If that happens, we will give God all the glory.

A Word About This Edition

This edition of the New International Reader's Version has been revised to include the changes of the New International Version. Over the years, many helpful changes have been made to the New International Version. Those changes were made because our understanding of the original writings is better. Those changes also include changes that have taken place in the English language. We wanted the New International Reader's Version to include those helpful changes as well. We wanted the New International Reader's Version to be as clear and correct as possible.

We want to thank the people who helped us prepare this new edition. They are Jeannine Brown from Bethel Seminary St. Paul, Yvonne Van Ee from Calvin College, Michael Williams from Calvin Theological Seminary, and Ron Youngblood from Bethel Seminary San Diego. We also want to thank the people at Biblica who encouraged and supported this work.

Kids, Read the Bible in a Whole New Way!

The Books of the Bible is a fresh way for kids to experience Scripture! Perfect for reading together as a family or church group, this 4-part Bible series removes chapter and verse numbers, headings, and special formatting. Now the Bible is easier to read, and reveals the story of God's great love for His people, as one narrative. Features the easy-to-read text of the New International Reader's Version (NIrV). Ages 8-12.

Look for all four books in *The Books of the Bible*:

Covenant History
Discover the Beginnings of God's People | 9780310761303

The Prophets
Listen to God's Messengers Tell about Hope and Truth | 9780310761358

The Writings
Learn from Stories, Poetry, and Songs | 9780310761334

New Testament
Read the Story of Jesus, His Church, and His Return | 9780310761310

My Bible Story Coloring Book
The Books of the Bible | 9780310761068

The Books of the Bible Children's Curriculum
9780310086161

These engaging lessons are formatted around relatable Scripture references, memory verses, and Bible themes. This curriculum has everything you need for 32 complete lessons for preschool, early elementary, and later elementary classes.

Read and Engage with Scripture in a Whole New Way!

The Books of the Bible is a fresh yet ancient presentation of Scripture ideal for personal or small group use. This 4-part Bible removes chapter and verse numbers, headings, and special formatting so the Bible is easier to read. The Bible text featured is the accurate, readable, and clear New International Version.

To get the entire Bible, look for all four books in *The Books of the Bible*:

Covenant History
Discover the Origins of God's People   9780310448037

The Prophets
Listen to God's Messengers Proclaiming Hope and Truth   9780310448044

The Writings
Find Wisdom in Stories, Poetry, and Songs   9780310448051

New Testament
Enter the Story of Jesus' Church and His Return   9780310448020

The Books of the Bible Study Journal   9780310086055

The Books of the Bible Video Study

9780310086109

Join pastor Jeff Manion and teacher John Walton as they look at the context and purpose for each book of the Bible. Included are (32) 10-minute sessions that can be used with large or small groups.